Men

Of

Merit

(Cover photograph:
a painting of Hesleyside, by Major John Charlton)

Men of Merit
- the life and works
of
John Dobson
(abridged version)
William Newton
John and Benjamin Green

by

H G Dobson (2006)

Written and published by H G Dobson

ISBN 0-9531840-7-2

Printed and bound by Martins the Printers Ltd,
Sea View Works, Spittal, Berwick upon Tweed.

Foreword

The Golden Age of Newcastle's – and Northumberland's – architecture was arguably the 19th century… give or take a decade; though these suggested parameters would, unfortunately, exclude the work of William Newton (1730-98) – an unforgivable omission.

There has never been, either before or since, an era in the city's long and proud history when so many gifted architects were simultaneously practising their profession and achieving so much.

"Men of Merit", has one fundamental objective; that of bringing to the attention of readers – with an interest in the fine architecture still extant in our region and, by means of photographic evidence, together with necessary but restrained explanatory text – some of the surviving achievements of four of these consummate artisans.

What the book does not purport to be (for space does not allow) is a complete, definitive chronicle of the many works attributed to these remarkable craftsmen. Neither is it, in the strictest interpretation of the word, a tome on architecture – in the vein of Nikolaus Pevsner's "Buildings of England" series – since it is conspicuously lacking the eminent professor's detailed, technical descriptions. To each their own; it is as well to recognise one's limitations. In any case, readers wishing to obtain this kind of specific information can quite easily consult specialist publications.

Inevitably, over the ensuing century and a half, a number of the fine buildings designed by these exceptional individuals, have sadly (one might say, shamefully) been destroyed; sacrificed, all too often, on the pitiless altar of 'progress', by complacent, even conceited 'guardians of the public interest' and ignorant barbarians masquerading as 'developers' anxious to 'improve' the built environment.

It can hardly be a coincidence that, proportionately, the works of the more successful members of this august brotherhood – John Dobson, William Newton, John and Benjamin Green – having largely survived the all too often destructive passage of time (outside the city's environs if not always within its limits), while those like David Stephenson, John and William Stokoe, Thomas and Andrew Oliver, John Wardle, etc – fine architects all, whose work has been grievously underestimated – have comparatively little to show for a lifetime of honest, dedicated labour.

Others, who practised mainly in the second half of the century and whose work has too often been neglected or ignored but which richly deserves far closer scrutiny, were also men of significant talent – the likes of Thomas Austin, John Johnstone, William B Parnell, Robert J Johnson and F W Rich – men who are now virtually forgotten, though fine examples of their work are still to be found both in Newcastle and the county of Northumberland.

But, I digress: let us therefore return to the four architects whose life and works are the subject of this present volume… the others, at a later date, may well be the topic of its sequel!

In "Men of Merit" it will quickly be apparent that I have not treated the work of my four subjects even-handedly… but with good reason. John Dobson, the most prodigious and gifted of this veritable galaxy of Newcastle's 19th century planners and technicians, has already been accorded the accolade (and justifiably so) of having books by several authors dedicated to his genius. In my own book, "Dobson on Dobson", for example, Dobson's work is graphically and fulsomely recorded. As the most prominent and celebrated of the four there has already been far more written about his extraordinary achievements than any or, indeed, all of the other three. To my knowledge, none of the others has shared or enjoyed this enviable distinction. Perhaps this is not entirely surprising since more of Dobson's work remains to be seen, in Newcastle, Northumberland and beyond, than the other three put together. Moreover, his work is generally considered to be of a superior quality. Doubtless, therefore, it is this combination of factors which, in part at least, accounts for his greater prestige and popularity.

"Men of Merit" consists of three parts: each is prefaced by a brief synopsis of the architect's life, and the works included are in alphabetical sequence *according to location.*

I have intentionally, and for reasons already explained, selected relatively few of Dobson's many works. Instead, I have opted to include some hitherto unpublished material.

In order to advertise the works of William Newton and John and Benjamin Green the constraints, already referred to, of available space, have regrettably imposed a degree of arbitrary selectivity and I have been compelled to omit some subjects already featured in others of my books.

Since Newton's output was not great my photographs of his surviving works represent an almost complete dossier.

Those illustrating the varied, and far more numerous, endeavours of the Greens – though necessarily selective – serve to portray, if not a complete record of their work, sufficient to demonstrate both their abilities and their versatility.

The professional reputations of Newton and the Greens have always been outshone by the brilliance of Dobson's career and resulting celebrity status – a modest, unassuming man rightly or wrongly regarded by many as the greatest architect ever to have lived and practised here, in the North-East of England. Indeed, there is no shortage of admirers who would assert that John Dobson was one of the most distinguished architects of his age, not just in a provincial context but by national standards also.

This particular volume, however, seeks simply (if at all possible) to redress this situation - however slightly - for while Dobson's stature is established, assured, unassailable, the others have struggled – largely without success - for any kind of recognition.

This modest offering seeks only to apportion a modicum of credit to the three less-well-known characters in this quartet of pre-eminent luminaries, in the hope that their valuable contribution to the architectural heritage of our region might be admitted and acknowledged.

Judge for yourselves, dear reader, from what you see and read, whether they, too, deserve the sobriquet, "Men of Merit".

Acknowledgements

I owe a sincere debt of gratitude to a great many people who assisted me in the production of this book, far too many to be listed individually: however, my special thanks are due to the following who kindly and graciously allowed me to photograph their properties.....

John Dobson

Wynyard Park (Sir John and Lady Hall); Blagdon Hall (The Hon. Matthew White Ridley); Gibside and Wallington Hall (The National Trust); Fallodon Hall (Mr P O R Bridgeman); Chesters (Mr George Benson); Bellister Castle and House (Mr and Mrs David Taylor and the National Trust); Blenkinsopp Hall (Mrs L M Joicey); Hexham House (Mr Alan Batey, Chief Executive of Tynedale Council); Minsteracres (Father Aelred Smith); Mitford Hall (Mr B S Shepherd); Hamsterley Hall (Mr T M Gibson); Cheeseburn Grange (Captain and Mrs S F Riddell).

William Newton

Hesleyside (Major F J Charlton); Capheaton (Mr John Browne-Swinburne); Castle Eden Hall (Mr Tony Gillman); Charlton Hall (Mr R W T Thorp); Craster Tower (Mr and Mrs J M Craster and Miss D M Cra'ster); Dissington Hall (Mr and Mrs Michael Brown); Acton House (Mr and Mrs D M Moore); Shawdon Hall (Major R F H Cowen); Howick Hall (Lord Howick of Glendale); Kielder Castle (Forest Enterprises); Lemmington Hall (Sir Charles Aitchison, Bart.); Close House and Fenham Hall (The University of Newcastle); Newton Hall (Mr and Mrs J I Patterson); Togston Hall (Mr Robert Gelley); Whitfield Hall (Mr and Mrs John Blackett-Ord).

John and Benjamin Green

Acklington Railway Station Master's House (Mr and Mrs D Charnock); Park Farm (His Grace the Duke of Northumberland); Ingram Farm (John and Sarah Wilson); The Literary and Philosophical Society (Members of the Committee); The Old Station, Norham (Mr and Mrs Peter Short); The Master Mariners' Homes (Hadaway & Hadaway, Solicitors (Reverend Timothy Duff); Secretaries to the Trustees); Lloyds Trustee Savings Bank (Mr Michael Rowland); Penshaw Monument (The National Trust); Styford Hall (Major R H Dickinson); St Bede Tower (The University of Sunderland); The Red Cottage (Mr Christopher Storey).

Index of colour plates:

Part One

John Dobson

Profile

John Dobson was born in the Pineapple Inn, in the village of High Chirton, now part of North Shields, on the 9th of December, 1787. He was the second of twelve children born to John and Margaret Dobson (née Clark). John Senior died c.1827; his wife a year later

John's father not only owned the inn but was a successful nurseryman, growing an abundance of excellent fruit and vegetables and, occasionally, he was employed to 'lay out' gardens, so that young John enjoyed a very comfortable childhood. His parents, having observed the lad's early talent for drawing nurtured the skill and not only gave him the advantage of a good education but granted him every facility to pursue his studies beyond his early years. At the age of fifteen he was apprenticed to David Stephenson, architect to Newcastle Corporation, whose 'crowning glory' was the Church of All Saints, still standing at the bottom of Pilgrim Street at the north end of the Tyne Bridge. Dobson spent eight years as an apprentice during which time he acquired not only a thorough knowledge of architecture but also the rudiments of masonry and carpentry. During this period he also studied surveying with a Mr Hall of Stamfordham and the arts of perspective, enamel painting and even fencing with an Italian refugee, Boniface Moss.

At the age of twenty-three Dobson set off for London, where he was to study watercolour painting with John Varley, "the father of watercolour drawing". He spent a year in the capital and struck up friendships with a number of notable men, including the Smirke brothers, Robert and Sydney – the latter of whom was to become his son-in-law. Robert Smirke (and others) strongly urged him to establish himself as an architect in London but young Dobson resisted their advice and returned to Newcastle. John Dobson was, by nature, a shy, retiring character and no doubt felt he would be a 'fish out of water' in the great metropolis. However, he was also astute enough to realise there were already a great number of aspiring young architects in London and therefore, as his mentor, Stephenson, had already suggested, his opportunities for success in his chosen profession were considerably greater in the north-east of England. In 1816 he married Isabella Rutherford of Gateshead, a lady of no mean artistic ability. They produced eight children though only their two eldest sons and daughters survived into adulthood: Isabella was to marry Sydney Smirke; Margaret Jane was to write 'the Memoir' of her father, in 1885; John Junior was to begin his career as a Master Mariner and though he helped his father for a while with administrative duties in the Pilgrim Street office he showed no inclination to continue the practice after his father died.

John's younger son, Alexander Ralph, was a brilliant young man who had clearly inherited the prodigious artistic talents of both his parents. Unfortunately, the promise of a glittering future came to a sudden and untimely end when Alexander was tragically killed in the Great Fire of 1854. It was said by many that John Dobson never fully recovered from the death of his gifted son.

In 1862 John Dobson suffered a severe stroke and on the 8th of January 1865, he died peacefully at his home in New Bridge Street, in the heart of Newcastle. He is buried in Jesmond's General Cemetery – which he had designed in 1834-6.

Many moving tributes were paid to this remarkable man of genius. It says much of this modest and honourable character that "there was never an architect more trusted alike by employer and employed: he never (once) exceeded an estimate and never had a legal dispute with a contractor".

This lovely little church, near Shotley Bridge, in the Early English style, is by John Dobson (1849-50). The tower has a 'broach spire' like that on another of Dobson's churches; St Cuthbert's on Bensham Road, Gateshead.

The first mention of the building is in the 1415 Survey, though the estate was granted to Sir Walter de Selby, by King Edward I, way back in the 13th century. It was also mentioned in the survey of 1509 ("Bedylsden") and again in the Survey drawn up at Newcastle on Tyne on December 2nd, 1541 – 'At Byttylsden Ys a toure & a barm kyn of the Inherytaunce of Percyvall Selby esqui' in good recap'ons & nere unto the same ys an other lytle toure at a place called the Cotte walles in measurable good recap'ons of the said p'cyvalle Selbyes Inheritaunce'.

By 1584 the spelling had changed yet again and was now "Bittlesden".

The Hall, situated north-east of Alwinton, on a slope of the Cheviot Hills some 800 feet above sea-level, remained in the possession of the Selby family for almost seven hundred years until the house and the estate were put up for sale in 1914 (*it was then withdrawn from sale as the best offer; was a paltry £11,000).

In 1787 the estate became the property of Thomas Selby. Thomas had married a wealthy heiress whose great fortune gave him free rein and c.1796 he rebuilt what had originally been a simple tower (the likes of which are to be found all over Northumberland) and created a mansion of splendid proportions. Outwardly quite plain in appearance, the Hall was a two-storeyed square block, six bays by five, the exterior only relieved by a fine, pedimented Tuscan porch. Inside, however, there were thirteen bedrooms, a dining room 27ft by 20ft; a drawing room and library each 31ft by 21ft and a massive billiards room measuring 43ft by 22 ft.

John Dobson was employed c.1820, by Walter Selby, when the house was much altered. To the north of the hall the old tower house was converted into a private chapel (- the Selbys were a staunch Roman Catholic family) late in the 19th century.

From 1925 the brewing magnate, Farquhar Deucher, lived at Biddlestone and during World War Two it was used as a convalescent home.

Sadly, the Hall was demolished c.1957 and only the chapel now survives.

Biddlestone's 'claim to fame' is that it is believed to be the Osbaldistone Hall featured in Sir Walter Scott's novel, 'Rob Roy'.

John Dobson was employed by Lord Londonderry in 1832 and, again, according to accounts in the Durham County Records Office, in 1838. Neville Whittaker (The Old Halls and Manor Houses of Durham) states that the Marquis again employed Dobson, in 1845, to carry out some of the necessary repairs and restoration after the fire in 1841.

Photographed by kind permission of Sir John and Lady Hall.

The east front has thirteen bays and is two storeys high with a balustraded parapet. The giant six-column Corinthian portico is two columns deep.

The foundation stone was laid in 1822 and the work was almost complete when, in 1841, a disastrous fire broke out. The repairs and restoration, it is said, cost just less than half the original cost of more than £100,000.

Photographed by kind permission of Sir John and Lady Hall.

The south front, facing the lake, is the original 18th century house belonging to the Tempests – a rich, coal-owning family.

In 1819, Lady Jane Vane-Tempest married Lord Stewart (who later became Marquis of Londonderry) and it was the Marquis who decided to 'rebuild on palatial lines'.

Blagdon Hall (Northumberland)

The manor of Blagdon (formerly Blakedene) was held in the Barony of Morpeth, by John de Plessis, in the reign of Henry III (1207-72). In 1567 it belonged to the Fenwickes, who later sold it to the Whites – a family who came from Hawthorn, in County Durham.

Matthew White amassed a considerable fortune as a merchant in Newcastle and it was he who built the present Hall (incorporating a little of its 17th century predecessor), between 1735-40.

The house was enlarged and ornamented by Matthew's son, Matthew Junior, who had been created a baronet in 1756.

A marriage between the Whites and the Ridleys united the two families. When Matthew (the first baronet) died, without issue, the estate passed to his sister Elizabeth, wife of Matthew Ridley of Heaton. Their son became the second baronet, Sir Matthew White Ridley, and ever since then heirs to the title have all borne the name Matthew White Ridley.

An old engraving of the east front of the Hall shows it as a two-storeyed building with heavy pilasters and a balustraded parapet. A second phase of work was completed c.1752 (evidenced by the date on some surviving rainwater heads). A second storey was added to the east front and the south front was then built: this may have been the work of Daniel Garrett. The house was remodelled between 1778-91, by James Wyatt, making the early 18th century east front conformable with the south. Wyatt also built the stables (1791) and the south lodge (1786) – the north lodge (1887) is by Lish. The main gate-piers outside the south lodge entrance to the estate are topped by big carved bulls, painted white.

Additions were made and porticos added from designs by Bonomi, in 1826 and 1830, but these additions were largely erased by later changes. The pleasure grounds and gardens were laid out – including a beautiful, ornamental pond.

The Hall was severely damaged by fire, in 1944, and was restored in 1948-9 by Robert Lutyens (when Bonomi's work all but disappeared).

The east front: seven bays wide, still shows traces of its 18th century pilasters. The central doorway is by Robert Lutyens (1948-49).

The south front.

The central doorway, on the east front, is by Robert Lutyens (1948-49). Inside the open pediment the Ridley coat-of-arms, shield supported by two bulls and the family motto – Constans Fidei.

The west front of the Hall might charitably be described as ‘unprepossessing’. In the centre foreground of the photograph is the one-storey, three-bay attachment of c.1820.

The south front also has seven bays though it is distinguished by a central, three-bay pediment. The first floor windows are all pedimented with coats-of-arms and garlands. To the left of the Hall is a single-storey, three-bay addition of c.1820.

Blagdon Hall (Northumberland)

The very plain north wing is an addition of c.1820.

John Dobson was involved in this undertaking.

The garden was partly remodelled c.1938 by Sir Edwin Lutyens – including a 'canal', 580 feet long, set at right angles to the house and ending in a circular 'basin' with a statue of Milo, by John Graham Lough, in the centre.

James Wyatt built the south lodge in 1786. The gate-piers outside the lodge are topped by large carved bulls, painted white.

Gibside (Burnopfield, Newcastle upon Tyne)

The house, built between 1603-20, during the reign of James I but probably incorporating older parts, is essentially that built by William Blakiston. The Hall passed to Sir William Bowes through his marriage to Elizabeth Blakiston, in 1692, and thence to Sir William's third son, George Bowes, and later still, in 1767, to the ninth Earl of Strathmore.

It was enlarged on the north side, probably in the mid-18th century, and again, on the east side, in 1805.

Meadows and Waterson ('Lost Houses of County Durham': Jill Raines, 1993) refer to John Dobson's plans for the addition of a conservatory for the tenth earl, writing that 'in 1813, Dobson made designs for an ambitious conservatory adjoining the house in a ...castellated manner'. The Earl had commissioned John Dobson to design a large conservatory which was to be added to the west end of the house. This charming building, of cast-iron and glass, was to be fed by rainwater and heated by hot air from an adjacent furnace: it would be possible to walk directly from the house into the conservatory, full of luxuriant and exotic plants. Meadows and Waterson claim the work was never done though 'his drawings of Gibside provide evidence for its appearance and plan at that date'.

In 1814 John Dobson proposed 'minor alterations' (- Lyall Wilkes describes them as 'large' and quotes 1813, 1815 and 1856 when work was carried out by the Newcastle architect). The Newcastle Daily Journal also mentions work done in 1856: in its obituary of January 16th, 1865, it says that Dobson made alterations to the 17th century house, for W Hutt MP, some nine years or so before the architect's death (in 1865).

The drawings referred to, relating to the proposed conservatory, are to be found in the Durham County Records Office (D/St/X46a,81), but an account also exists in that same office for "unknown work", in 1818, for which John Dobson was paid the sum of £50 (D/St/V1513, pp14-15).

The south front was rebuilt by John Bowes (the tenth Earl), who removed the third storey and replaced the front with a high battlemented parapet (- work by Alexander Gilkie), pierced with huge crosses.

Nevertheless, the careful reconstruction of the main porch and the character of the five bays, of square mullioned windows, denotes a sympathetic respect for Jacobean architecture.

After the death of the wife of the tenth Earl (mother of John Bowes), in 1860, the house was little used.

After the death of John Bowes, in 1885, the house was never again occupied by the family.

The late Queen Elizabeth the Queen Mother recalled occasional picnics being taken at Gibside, at the beginning of the twentieth century, but obviously these would be held in the grounds of the house.

In 1889 there had been plans mooted to convert the Hall into a hydropathical establishment but nothing came of them. Land Army girls were billeted in the house during the 1914-18 war but by then its roof was failing and it lacked both plumbing and sanitation.

It was gutted in 1920 and a large fireplace... supporting a large mantel, decorated with the Blakeston arms, was transferred to Glamis Castle, where it was installed in the billiards room.

'The house at Gibside is today forlorn… roofless and decaying.'

Gibside has been a roofless shell since 1920 but 'it still preserves the character of a long, low, Jacobean-style building capped by an exaggeratedly high castelled parapet'.

The wing added in 1805, to the right of the main entrance, was probably by David Stephenson, Newcastle's leading architect at that time.

Photographed by kind permission of the National Trust.

The entrance porch, though reconstructed in 1805, probably represents the 17th century porch, with Tuscan columns on high pedestals, the Royal Arms of James I flanked by sculpted figures… the initials of William and Jane Blakiston and the date 1620.

Photographed by kind permission of the National Trust.

Wallington Hall

In the 16th century a Tudor house was added to the existing medieval castle already occupying the site, by 'Sir John Fenwicke'.

The last of the Fenwicks, (Cavaliers and Jacobites) to own Wallington was Sir John Fenwick, who was executed in 1697 on a charge of plotting to kill King William III.

Some years previously, however, the house had been purchased from Sir John (-by now a 'landless and broken man') by Sir William Blackett who, immediately on purchase of the estate demolished both castle and Tudor house and, in 1688, began the construction of the present building – modelled on a French chateau.

The house remained the possession of the Blacketts until 1777 when, on the death of Sir Walter Blackett (who died childless but whose only sister, Julia, had married Sir George Trevelyan, in 1733) the estate passed into the hands of the Trevelyan's – a Cornish family by origin. Sir William Trevelyan owned Wallington from 1846-79. At that time the house surrounded a damp, dark and dingy courtyard.

John Dobson was presumably chosen, in 1855, to convert the courtyard into useable living space because of his years of experience with the houses of the Trevelyan's neighbours.. Angerton, Mitford, Meldon etc. Dobson's design was in a subdued Italianate style, thoroughly appropriate to the rest of the house (described as one of the most beautiful 18th century houses in Northumberland), though 'the hall impinges little on the older rooms, with their exceptionally fine 18th century plasterwork'. Only the staircase had to be rebuilt to accommodate the 'hall', which rises in two tiers of arcades towards a coffered ceiling.

It was John Ruskin, who had suggested the courtyard should be roofed over and the present, beautifully-lighted picture gallery (or hall) was created under Ruskin's directions.

Indeed, John Dobson's designs had to be submitted to Ruskin for his approval as he, Ruskin, was Lady Pauline Trevelyan's mentor 'in all things artistic'. It would be interesting to know what Dobson's thoughts were regarding this arrangement but, perhaps wisely, he kept them to himself.

The pictures, painted between 1856-60, around the north and south walls of the gallery are all by William Bell Scott, a pre-Raphaelite artist who, at the time of his work at Wallington, had been Master of the Government School of Design, in Newcastle, since 1843.

The eight paintings portray scenes from Northumberland's history throughout the centuries, starting with the Roman Wall.

Like Lady Waterford's paintings in Ford Village Hall Scott featured local people (some celebrated, others from ordinary walks of life) in several of his pictures. For example, in his picture, 'building the Roman Wall', the centurion is a portrait of John Clayton, of Chesters, Newcastle's Town Clerk. Another character portrayed on the same canvas is Dr John Collingwood Bruce, the recognised authority on all things related to the Roman Wall.

Mr William Henry Charlton, of Hesleyside, is portrayed in 'The Spur in the Dish', a scene in a Border castle anytime during the Middle Ages. A friend of Scott's, one Miss Boyd, appears on both 'the Spur...' and 'Grace Darling' – whereon she represents the Longstone heroine, helping her father, William, rescue the survivors of the Forfarshire, wrecked on Harcar Rock, in 1838.

Scott, himself, appears in a painting titled, 'Bernard Gilpin' and Lady Pauline features in 'The Descent of the Danes'.

But others, perhaps less instantly recognisable, were also used as 'models' – a clergyman and a porter in, 'King Egfrid and Cuthbert', a gamekeeper and a piper, in 'The Spur in the Dish', and three figures hammering, in 'Iron and Coal', were men from George Stephenson's workshop on Tyneside. John Ruskin is said to have designed the balustrade on the first floor. The stone pilasters between the paintings were decorated with cats and wheat and blue cornflowers by Lady Pauline Trevelyan (neé Jermyn), a 'brilliant and sensitive woman', her friends and the ubiquitous Ruskin. The upper spandrels depict the Border Ballad of Chevy Chase, while the lower spandrels portray the heads of eminent men who have made an impression, of one kind or another, on our County's long and glorious history... among whom are shown the Emperors Hadrian and Severus (who built and repaired the Wall); Alcuin (a brilliant scholar at the court of Charlemagne); Bishop Ridley (-burnt at the stake for his religious beliefs, in 1555); the Earl of Derwentwater (- beheaded in 1716 for his part in the Jacobite Rebellion the previous year); Nathaniel Crewe (- a notorious time-serving Bishop...of Durham... of whom it was said, 'he was neither a brilliant political nor ecclesiastical character and there was nothing in his life became him like the leaving of it, since he then founded the Bamburgh Trust'.): Admiral Lord Collingwood (- of Trafalgar fame); John and William Scott (- later Earl Eldon and the Lord Chancellor of England and his brother, Lord Stowell); Thomas Bewick (- the celebrated engraver); Earl 'Reform Bill' Grey (- whose statue stands on a pedestal a the top of Grey Street – which was also renamed in his honour) and George Stephenson (- the 'Father of the Railway').

In 1928, Sir Charles Trevelyan, a noted socialist and member of two Labour governments – in 1924 and 1929 – inherited Wallington Hall. In 1936 he declared his intention of leaving, on his death, the estate of Wallington to the National Trust; on condition that his wife and children should be entitled to continue to reside at Wallington, as tenants, during their lives. Sir Charles died in 1958.

The Clock Tower

Wallington Hall (Cambo, Northumberland)

The house was built for Sir William Blackett in 1688, on the site of an earlier house owned by the Fenwicks.

The gargoyles on the east lawn to the front entrance of the house are said to have come from one of London's City Gates, which were rebuilt after the Great Fire of 1666. The story is that they were used as ballast in one of Blackett's coal-boats returning north to the Tyne.

Photographed by kind permission of the National Trust.

In the first half of the 17th century a Puritan merchant from Berwick named Sakeld, built a small country house at Fallodon. In 1704 Thomas Wood bought the estate and c.1730 he pulled down Sakeld's house and built a red-brick mansion – the bow on the south side is a later addition (c.1796?). After Wood's death in 1755 the house passed to the Grey family and it was during the occupancy of Sir Edward Grey (later Viscount Grey of Fallodon) that the building was practically destroyed by fire, in May 1917: Grey painstakingly restored his beloved home, brick by brick, in the same style as before but with two storeys instead of the previous three.

Photographed by kind permission of Mr Peter O R Bridgeman.

Fallodon Hall (Christon Bank, Northumberland)

The east wing (right) is of dressed sandstone and was added by John Dobson in 1815 though why he used sandstone and not red brick, in keeping with the rest of the house remains a mystery. The bow, on the south elevation, was added at the end of the 18th century.

The stable-block, also of sandstone is likely to have been Dobson's work.

Photographed by kind permission of Mr Peter O R Bridgeman.

Fallodon Hall (Christon Bank, Northumberland)

The east wing (left of centre) was added by John Dobson in 1815, though why he used dressed, pink sandstone instead of red brick has never been explained.

The kitchen wing (facing north), where Viscount Grey was obliged to live for some years after the disastrous fire of 1917, was re-fronted in 18th century brick and incorporates part of the 17th century house first built on the site by a Puritan merchant from Berwick named Samuel (?) Sakeld. In 1924 the main block was completely remodelled when the Hall's second floor was removed.

Photographed by kind permission of Mr Peter O R Bridgeman.

The Church of St Cuthbert (Greenhead, Northumberland)

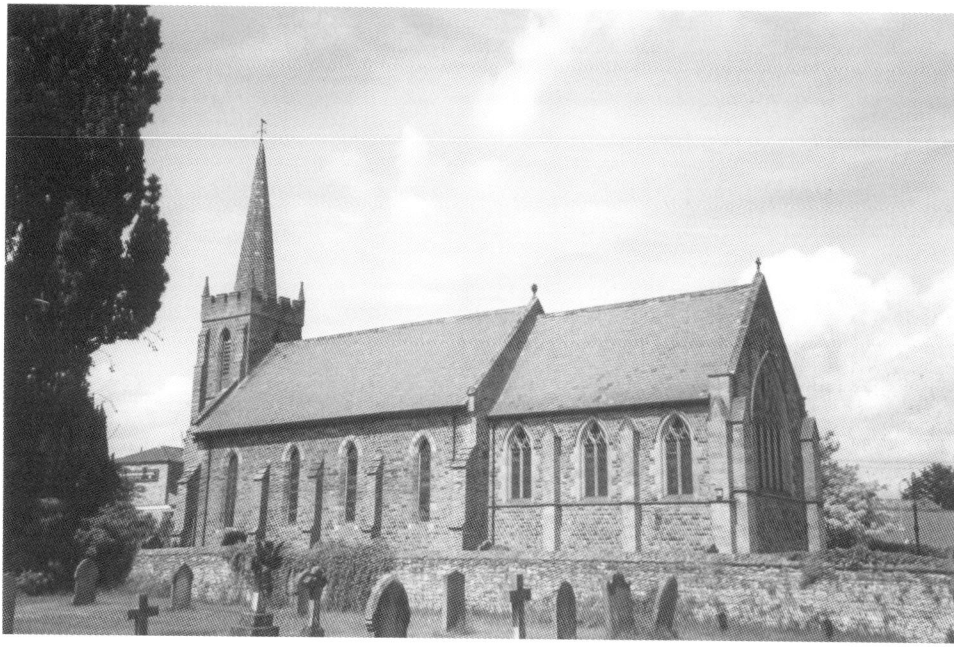

Designed by John Dobson and built between 1826-28, St Cuthbert's is a small, rectangular church with a slender octagonal spire.

Built of local stone, in the Early English style, it was partly paid for by Nathaniel Hollingsworth, a local poet who became Vicar of Haltwhistle.

In the Border Survey of 1541 it was described as a "bastell-house", occupied by the Blenkinsopps and kept in good repair. Stone from the Roman Wall was used in its construction. A date-plate of 1669 indicates a hall addition to the medieval tower but the residential house dates from the 19th century with the mullioned windows and two embattled tower-like projections.

The house overlooks the gardens, the ruined part overlooks the approach and the parkland pastures.

Bellister Castle and House (Haltwhistle, Northumberland)

Bellister was described as a "bastle house", which suggests it was more a pele tower than a Castle. The old pele tower is now a roofless ruin: the adjacent house was added by John Kirsopp but remodelled by John Dobson, in 1827 (when he also added the first floor windows, either side of the centre block, on the south side). The house was altered again, c.1890, and again, in 1900, after a devastating fire.

In 1975 it was given to the National Trust. The present occupants have lived here since 1987.

The south side of the Tower.

John Kirsopp added the modern house (above) which was remodelled by John Dobson in 1827. It was occupied until 1975 when it was given to the National Trust. The present occupants have lived here since 1987.

Featured, on the first floor either side of the centre-block, are two of "Mr Dobson's windows".

Photographed by kind permission of both the National Trust and the present occupants, David and Grethe Taylor.

Blenkinsopp Hall (Haltwhistle, Northumberland)

It is said that early in the 19th century the Hall was largely rebuilt with a long, two layered south front of five bays and that John Dobson (possibly) added a south-east tower together with other substantial additions. Despite assertions that these additions have since been demolished Mrs L M Joicey, in a letter to me dated August 17th, 1998, writes… 'The part that was pulled down in 1950 was only built c.1899 so if the earlier part was built by John Dobson then most of it survives'.

Photographed by kind permission of Mrs L M Joicey.

Large additions were made to the Hall, including a south-east tower, for Colonel J B Coulson, c.1835. Substantial later additions were made c.1877-80.

Dobson's tower has indeed been demolished. The castellated porch which is there now was added by Edward Joicey, in 1877.

Photographed by kind permission of Mrs L M Joicey.

The Priory and Parish Church of St Andrew (Hexham, Northumberland)

Not all of John Dobson's work met with universal acclaim and admiration. Reconstruction work on St Nicholas' Cathedral (Parish Church, as it then was) led to his being taken to task by his fellows in the Newcastle Society of Antiquaries. Rebuilding work done at St Gregory's, Kirknewton was vehemently opposed by his hitherto friend and supporter, the distinguished architect Anthony Salvin. His restoration work on the Church of St Michael and All Angels, Ford, has been criticised for 'having obliterated many of the most interesting features' and for 'over-restoring the church'.

But perhaps his most controversial piece of restoration work, arousing much vociferous opposition, was carried out on Hexham Abbey.

He had been engaged in work of one kind or another, on St Andrew's, since 1817 and in 1828 he restored the Abbey's east window, overlooking the Market Place. In 1858, however, he finally removed the unusual late Gothic, five-light structure, with a 'rose' as its centrepiece and replaced it with two tiers of triple lancets, a design based on that at Whitby Abbey. Pevsner describes the result as "disappointing".

Faulkener & Greg described the effect as "hard, neat and academically correct", adding that, although it was approved by many of his colleagues "it was censured by some of the journals of the time in the severest terms". W W Tomlinson it even more incensed and writes that "the Abbey has suffered much from destructive restoration". He adds that "Vandals have impaired the Gothic beauty. The east end was restored in a barbarous manner…."

The Newcastle Daily Chronicle of January 9th, 1865, gives a somewhat different version of the 'facts'…

"In 1817, Dobson was called in by Colonel Beaumont to restore the east end of Hexham Abbey Church. Dobson urged that the East end, a fine example of the early pointed style, should be restored in harmony with the rest of the building, but his design was overruled and the Catherine Wheel window of a late and debased style was consequently replaced.

Dobson, thirty years later, demolished his own work and restored the harmony of the building by introducing two tiers of lancet windows similar to the Abbey Church in Whitby, which Dobson considered of the same approximate date."

The east gable of the Priory, overlooking the Market Place.

The Reverend Thomas Andrews was lecturer at Hexham Abbey from 1717-57 and he it was who built the house in gardens purchased from one Mrs Dorothy Shafto. The original house was of five bays and had narrow windows but was much smaller than the present building.

In 1757 the house passed to Thomas' brother, Robert, and in 1764 it passed again to Robert's daughter, Honour, who had married the Reverend Sloughter Clarke. In 1801 it became the property of their son, the Reverend Robert Clarke – also a lecturer at the Abbey. Robert Clarke made a number of dramatic additions and alterations to the house. He added the third storey, the porch (on square pillars) facing the garden, and both the east and west wings. The house was occupied by the Reverend Canon Barker (another lecturer) until the late 19th century. In 1915 a Miss Illingworth moved her school here, from Scarborough, when that town was bombarded by the Germans. In 1918 the house was bought by a Mr Tully until, eventually, in 1926, it was sold to Hexham Urban Council, for use as a public library. Three years later the gardens were turned into a public park and bowling green.

The house is now used as offices by Tynedale Council.

The house was built in 1771 by John Errington. The architect was John Carr of York.

The fourth edition of Archaelogia Aeliana (vol. XXXVI) tells that, in 1832 and 1837 alterations were carried out by John Dobson, for John Clayton. These may well have taken the form of the addition of an arcade to the north entrance, a central doorway on the south side and alterations to the windows in the wings.

Photographed by kind permission of Mr George Benson.

Minsteracres Monastery (Kiln Pit Hill, near Consett, Co. Durham)

Albert Silvertop bought the land at Minsteracres, in 1725, but it was George Silvertop, while living in Stella, who built up the family's fortune in the coal trade – with shares in mines at Greenside, Winlaton and Blagdon – and it was he who added most of the land to the estate.

His son, John, built the present mansion between 1780 and 1800, on the site of an earlier house of which nothing now remains except (perhaps) the lodges and the stables.

Tomlinson writes: "The Hall is a fine stately building and was improved and enlarged (in 1866-7) by the addition of a north wing".

Elsewhere it is described as 'a large, informal house'.

A Roman Catholic Chapel, in the Gothic style and dedicated to St Elizabeth, was added in 1852-54 to replace the oratory. This small chapel was built on the instructions of Henry Silvertop (who had changed his name from Englefield). His wife, Eliza, laid the foundation stone in September 1852 and the church was dedicated to the Bishop of Hexham, on August 24th, 1854.

Successive members of the family lived in Minsteracres until, in 1952, Charles sold the house and the parkland to a religious order – the Passionists. Minsteracres had finally, after more than a century and a half, passed out of the hands of the Silvertop family.

A second floor was added to the house at the beginning of the nineteenth century.

The building is approached up a long avenue of magnificent, giant redwood trees and is now the property of the Passionists – a religious Order.

John Dobson made large additions to the house, in 1816, for George Silvertop: these are believed to include the large bay-window and the colonnade, on the left.

Photographed by kind permission of Father Aelred Smith.

Minsteracres Monastery (Kiln Pit Hill, near Consett, Co Durham)

Statue of Our Lady of Minsteracres with the Church of St Elizabeth.

Photographed by kind permission of Father Aelred Smith.

The house was designed by John Dobson in 1823 but not built until 1828. It is surely one of Dobson's most beautiful creations. Described as a 'handsome, square building, rather plain but relying for effect on the quality of the stonework – the beautiful white sandstone was obtained from the River Font'.

Hodgson added: 'The site is well chosen. This is a fertile and most delightful place'.

Photographed by kind permission of Mr B S Shepherd.

'At the east end of Grey Street, we find the entire length distributed into five architectural compartments, separated by the crossing of other streets. The first, or southern compartment, from Mosely Street to Shakespeare Street, has in the centre a colonnade of lofty Corinthian columns with wings having pilasters and balustrades….'

(The Northumberland Directory: 1854)

'The second storey of the centre (of the east side of Grey Street) consists of a recessed range of lofty fluted columns of a Corinthian order, and the upper storey of which is adorned with a row of square vases. On each side of this centre is a house with projecting wings, the upper storeys supported by square pilasters, above which are elegant mouldings and the attics of the wings are surmounted by neat balustrades. A large window in the second storey of each wing is ornamented with a neat pediment in Italian style and a balustrade runs along the centre of the second storey from wing to wing. Ranges of buildings sweep off to the north and the south of the houses just noticed, terminated by projecting wings decorated in a nearly similar manner to the houses immediately flanking the centre. A similar style prevails on this side of the street after passing High Bridge to the corner of Shakespeare Street.'

(Architectural and Picturesque Views of Newcastle upon Tyne: Collard and Ross, 1847)

Even this detail fails to bring out the skill of the designer (architect) in maintaining architectural harmony and proportion, not only on a convex curve but also on a steeply rising slope which had to correspond exactly with the great sweep of the concave (ie the west side of the street). It is no wonder that excavations sometimes went as deep as thirty-five feet and that in some cases more masonry was buried underground than appeared in the whole elevation of the façade.

Norfolk House (80-96 Grey Street) (Newcastle upon Tyne)

A design of typical simplicity – short window pilasters and giant framing pilasters, the latter with Corinthian capitals.

This block has retained its balustrades; other buildings further down the street have not.

John Dobson's architecture on the east side of Grey Street is generally simpler and more subdued and perhaps less dramatic than John Wardle's west side. Sadly, however, much of Dobson's original work – from Norfolk House (Shakespeare Street) right down to Mosley Street – has (since 1836) been either repaired, restored, rebuilt or remodelled.

Numbers 52-78 include a small corner pavilion and a large, seven-window-wide pavilion separated by a plain section that was originally four houses. 52-60 were repaired and extended (to the rear of the premises) in 1996. The Edwardian shop front, of number 52, and the balustrade above number 60 were also restored at that time.

This was Dobson's "grand centre piece" already referred to.

Two thirds of the original façade, however, were demolished and rebuilt in 1910, in – as David Lovie describes it – 'a heavy and inappropriate classical style'.

Fortunately, in a 1969 restoration scheme these alterations were removed and everything except the ground floor was replaced in the style of Dobson's original work of c.1836: faithfully reproducing his columns, cornices, upper floor windows and even the decorative urns.

Grand pavilion and plain, two-house section. The large pavilion, once described as “a house with projection wings”, still retains its attic and first floor balustrade. The ground floor, using local natural stone ‘columns’, is a twentieth century alteration.

Another of John Dobson's 'grand pavilions'. This is far more decorative than his other pavilions on the street and while its appearance is extremely pleasing to the eye it is so out of character with Dobson's style it is more likely the work of W L Newcombe (another versatile local architect) who, in 1890, added an ornate late Victorian ground floor and extended the interior. Around 1981 further interior alterations were made.

- before restoration:

This was the last 'piece of the jigsaw' on Grey Street to be completed (on the junction with Mosley Street) and it required a grant from the Corporation, in 1842, for it to be so.

2-8 Grey Street (Newcastle upon Tyne)

- after restoration:

An 18th century building (with cellars) already occupied this corner site and it may be that rather than demolish it completely Grainger simply "tarted it up" – refurbishing the interior while Dobson used an elaborate Italian design to remodel the upper building. For many years it stood as an eyesore at the bottom of Grey Street (unused and unloved)... its restoration was finally completed c.2003.

'The Butcher and Green Markets (ie the present Grainger Market), with the block of houses enclosing them, were designed by the late Mr John Dobson…' – a statement expressed in the Newcastle Daily Chronicle, of March 21st, 1868, and which has never seriously been contradicted.

The east front of the Market has giant, fluted Corinthian pilasters on both the wings and the central pavilion. Such was the popularity of Grainger Street in the late 19th and 20th centuries that it became the main commercial street of the City. This inevitably led to a number of alterations, expansions and modifications to the properties… roofs were raised or flattened on several premises; shop fronts have been altered several times; canopies were added but, thankfully, later removed.

The west front of the Market follows the same pattern as the east, on Grainger Street, except here the eight bays on the central pavilion are plain and the fluted pilasters are conspicuously absent.

The north front of the Market follows Dobson's usual pattern of wings, plain links and pavilions.

Grainger Street and Clayton Street, being the town's principal streets, their architecture is more elaborate, more decorative. On Nelson Street only the wings have decorative pilasters, the rest is fairly plain.

The Market's south front on Nun Street is identical to that on Nelson Street; the giant pilasters are again confined to the end wings.

John Dobson's church of 1846 has three central windows above a moulded arch door. The gable is buttressed. Pevsner says the style is Romanesque: the Newcastle Daily Journal described it as 'neo-Norman'.

Described as "one of the most endearing of all Gothic houses in County Durham… it is the epitome of the late 18th century house, at its most genial and charming".

In 1762, Sir John Swinburne created the house substantially as we see it today, a medium- sized house representing a happy amalgam of Georgian and Gothic features. Yet, the Gothic features are minimal: the form of the upper windows and the fanciful bay-window with its "pretty pattern of glazing bars". "This is really", suggests Neville Whittaker, "Gothic fashion applied as decoration only, to the simple form of a Georgian house."

Photographed by kind permission of Mr T M Gibson.

On the death of Sir John Swinburne the house and estate passed to his brother, Henry – a man of great taste and, as an indefatigable traveller, of great experience. So perhaps it was natural he should select the fashionable Gothic style for the improvement of his house which, basically is a simple rectangle.

The pinnacle (left of the gate-post) is from the old Houses of Parliament: the cupola (on the right) is from the demolished mansion of Beaudesert, in Staffordshire.

In 1815, John Dobson made alterations to the Hall for R S Surtees: both a corn mill on the estate (1819) and the Handley Cross Bridge, of 1815, are also believed to be the work of John Dobson.

In 1813 John Dobson carried out numerous alterations to the house for Ralph Riddell: the front door was moved from the south side to the west (featured); he altered the windows and added the tower over the front door. The west front is now two-storeyed with tripartite windows. The tall, castellated centre bay has a castellated porch. Dobson also added the private Roman Catholic chapel (left).

At the same time as he remodelled the house John Dobson also laid out the grounds 'in a characteristically early 19th century Picturesque manner'.

Photographed by kind permission of Captain and Mrs S F Riddell.

The bridge, designed by John Dobson, crosses the River Eden on the A69 trunk road from Hexham to Carlisle and divides the villages of Warwick Bridge on the east side from Warwick on the west.

Brick built, it has three fine, wide, segmental arches.

Pevsner and Faulkner and Greg all cite 1837 as the year of its construction yet the date stone clearly shows it was built, by William Denton, between 1833-35.

In 1859, Dobson was elected first President of the newly formed Northern Architectural Association.

In 1862 he suffered a severe stroke which left him partly paralysed and from which he never recovered, this, effectively brought to an end his formidable active working life. He moved to Ryton where, it was hoped, the country air might benefit his health. At the end of December, 1864, however, he returned with his daughter to his home in New Bridge Street where he died on Sunday, January 8th, 1865.

The Newcastle Daily Journal paid him the following tribute:

'... there are few buildings of any note, in this town or in Northumberland, with which his name is not, in some way, associated: ... it may be questioned whether any architect, in London or the provinces, has ever designed... such a number of buildings and of such a miscellaneous character.'

John Grundy described him as 'The most prominent and most talented of the group... of local architects who emerged in the early part of the 19th century.' Tom Faulkner and Andrew Greg wrote: 'Dobson brought to the region London's most fashionable ideas together with a Geordie's down-to-earth practicality'.

Hesleyside (Bellingham, Northumberland)

1. The lovely two-and-a-half storey, seven-bay east front with its slightly projecting, pedimented, three-bay centre.

2. The magnificent portico.

Wallington Hall (Cambo, Northumberland)

3. In 1855 the courtyard was roofed in and given an Italian arcade on square pillars and an arched gallery. The architect was John Dobson.

Photograph included by kind permission of the National Trust.

4. The very attractive south front clearly showing the hood moulded windows, the crenellated parapet and the rather odd (and somewhat conspicuous) corner turrets.

The south end of the 'palm house' is attached on the left.

5. The south and east fronts.

Hexham House (Hexham, Northumberland)

6. The house, now offices belonging to Tynedale Council, was built at the beginning of the 18th century and altered by John Dobson for T R Beaumont in 1819

7. The Priory seen from the gardens of Hexham House.

8. When the main entrance to the Hall was transferred from the south side to the north, at the beginning of the nineteenth century (1809) a one-storey Tuscan addition was made for the entrance hall.

9. The pediment is supported by the giant Iconic columns, paired at either end of the central block. The windows of the wings, set in their semi-circular arches, reflect the building's neo-classical taste.

The front is marred by an incongruous and rather tasteless twentieth century canopy.

10. The main entrance on William Newton's north front, with its four giant Tuscan columns and pediment.

11. The pedimented south front and pedimented doorway..

12. Built as almshouses, in 1837, by John and Benjamin Green, on land provided by the Third Duke of Northumberland, whose statue can be seen at the top of the steps and in front of the clock tower, facing the River Tyne… for the Tyne Mariners' Benevolent Institution.

Penshaw Monument (Penshaw, County Durham)

13. Penshaw Hill makes a prominent landmark surmounted as it is by a Greek-style temple, marking the place where the Lambton Worm is said to have "lapped its tail".

The column stands on a stylobate (ie a solid platform on which a colonnade stands) but there are no steps and no inscriptions.

The building itself is not very imposing, but seen at a distance it attracts attention.

14. A medium-sized house of c.1770, described as "…the epitome of the late 18th century house at its most genial and charming".

15. The Tudor-style chimney stacks are truly a work of art.

16. The south front and garden.

The second storey and balustrade were added in 1856 and all the windows were altered.

Part Two

William Newton

Profile

William Newton was born in 1730, in Newcastle, and was christened at St Andrew's Church, Newgate Street, on the 20th of December that same year. Very little is known of his early life.

He was the son of Robert Newton, a shipwright, who turned his attention to architecture and who practised as a builder-architect in Newcastle.

Around the year 1760 William built the castellated Castle Eden for Edward Burdon, later described rather unkindly as 'a rather dull piece of gothic painting'.

In 1762-3 he and his father carried out repairs to the Church of St Mungo, at Simonburn, in Northumberland.

In 1763 he married Dorothy Bell of Gateshead who bore him no fewer than twelve children – six sons and six daughters.

His first substantial work appears to have been St Ann's Church in the Sandgate area of Newcastle, off City Road. Built between 1764-8, at the expense of the Corporation, both to replace the decayed, medieval building formerly occupying the site and as a chapel-of-ease for All Saints Church, on Pilgrim Street: it has been described as 'a small but attractive church in the well-established Georgian tradition' – ie it has a rectangular nave with large, round-headed windows and an elegant tower and spire at the west end, embellished with urns.

"The only possible fault," opines the 'Tyneside Classical Tradition', "is that the small-scale, Tuscan portico sits rather uncomfortably against the large, blank, west wall and pediment."

A drawing by Newton for Newcastle's Lunatic Asylum (of 1765-77) is in the Northumberland County Records Office. It had a plain, rectangular, brick façade embellished only with string courses and a pedimented door case. For him to be in the enviable, financial position whereby he could afford to take a lease, from Newcastle Corporation, on the piece of land ultimately to be called Charlotte Square, Newton must already have had a number of rewarding commissions under his belt by 1769.

Colvin claims Newton did have a "considerable local practice", but whether this was prior to 1769 or subsequent to the purchase of the lease, Colvin doesn't make clear.

No matter: he acquired the land and a number of substantial brick houses, 'to a minimum size specified by the Corporation', were duly constructed on three sides of the site – indeed, Newton and his family lived in one of the houses for twenty years.

Why Newton was awarded the contract to design the Assembly rooms is not known: one can only speculate. What is known is that the Chairman of the Assembly Rooms Committee, William Lowes, was a great friend of Newton's early patron, Rowland Burdon (of Castle Eden), but to draw any kind of conclusion from this coincidence could be construed as uncharitable, to say the least. The fact is that when building began, in 1774, William Newton was the only really talented architect in the whole of Newcastle and so, perhaps the Committee had little alternative, under these circumstances, but to award the contract to him.

There is, moreover, little doubt that the success of this project enhanced Newton's reputation considerably and led to profitable subsequent contracts from the 'local gentry' and a number of country house commissions which might very well not otherwise have come his way.

William Newton has been dismissed as a 'conventional Georgian architect whose work is sometimes elegant, always pleasing but never remarkable'. In 'The Buildings of England: Northumberland' (1992 edition), we are told that while 'he was clearly very competent, he was not a great architect'. Neville Whittaker describes him as a 'provincial classicist – albeit one of the first order…'

In 'The Tyneside Classical Tradition' we read – 'Newton's houses were not all identical… the few that remain today remind us that the mid-18th century saw the beginning of a new prosperity in the North East'.

Castle Eden, built for Rowland Burdon, is described as 'a rather dull piece of Gothic scene painting'.

Whitifield, parts of Hesleyside and Dissington are said to be no more than 'relatively plain houses, relying for their effect on the quality of their splendid stonework'.

Acton House, Felton, near Morpeth, however, is described by Pevsner (1992) as 'quite a grand house….' and Shawdon Hall (very probably designed by Newton) as 'one of the finest neoclassical houses in the area'.

Even St Ann's Church, on City Road, Newcastle, is not entirely free from criticism. Pevsner states that it is 'a stately classical church… with a plain and well-designed west tower'. Allsopp and Clark describe it as 'a civilised and charming little building'. The note of dissent is introduced in 'The Tyneside Classical Tradition' which writes that though 'it is a small but attractive church… its small scale Tuscan portico sits rather uncomfortably against the large blank west wall and pediment'. One thing his critics do agree upon is the quality of Newton's Assembly Rooms, on Fenkle Street, Newcastle.

Quoting again from 'The Tyneside Classical Tradition' it is fulsome in its praise. 'His design, inside and out, is supremely elegant… all its features reflect its neoclassical taste'. 'The interior', it continues, '… is a superb example of provincial decorative design … and… the finest neo-domestic interior in the region'.

E Mackenzie, writing way back in 1827, said, 'This monument… is remarkable for the elegance of design and the execution of workmanship'.

Bruce Allsopp and Ursula Clark describe it as '…the finest building of its kind and period in Britain'. They believe it compares favourably with its counterpart in Bath and is 'both more elegant and more spacious… than York'.

Frank Graham's opinion is more restrained. Nevertheless he declares it to be '… one of the finest buildings in Newcastle'.

The only comment made in the 1992 edition of 'The Buildings of England: Northumberland' is that it is designed 'in a fine Adamish style'.

No doubt all of these opinions of Newton's work and his abilities as an architect are worthy of note. There was, I am sure, no malice in the minds and judgement of his critics and certainly it is true there is more value attached to balanced and informed opinion than simple emotional appraisal. Laymen, like myself, lack the technical expertise needed to evaluate architecture and to decide what is and what is not 'good' architecture, but I am sure, nonetheless, that even with or without technical qualification we are perfectly capable of deciding what is 'elegant'.

Whether Newton was a 'great' architect or whether his architecture was 'remarkable' I am unable to say. Few architects, I imagine, are worthy of the term 'great': fewer still can be said to be 'remarkable'.

John Dobson is probably the 'greatest' architect this region has ever produced but he was not without his critics. Perhaps some of *his* work was 'remarkable' but I doubt whether Dobson's staunchest supporters would claim that all of *his* work was either 'great' or 'remarkable'.

Newton was the forerunner of a crop of very successful architects working in Newcastle throughout the nineteenth century.

One thinks of the Stokoes, William and John; John and Benjamin Green; of Thomas Oliver, John Wardle and George Walker – and, of course (though earlier and in the 18th century), his near contemporary, David Stephenson.

All of these men produced some work which many regard as having been of a very high (one is tempted to say excellent) standard, but not one of them, I venture to suggest, was able to sustain a standard of excellence throughout their careers and in every piece of work they did: to expect them to do so would have been totally unreasonable - even the celebrated Mr Dobson was incapable of achieving these dizzy heights of expectancy:

I am equally sure that the owners of Hesleyside, Capheaton, Lemmington, Backworth, Dissington and Whitfield were perfectly satisfied with the work carried out by William Newton as, no doubt, was The Duke of Northumberland at Kielder Castle, Sir Henry Grey at Howick, the Ords at Fenham Hall and the Newcastle Corporation with their 'civilised and charming church on City Road – if they were not I can find no record of their complaint.

Most people, I believe, 'know what they like', whether it be art, music, literature, fashion – or architecture.

They listen respectfully to the views of 'experts' but, in the final analysis they make up their own minds: sometimes, I suspect, they may even take a contumacious delight in 'cocking a snook' at the opinions of these so-called experts, whom they view (not without some good reason) with both scepticism and downright suspicion.

Perhaps the fact that most of Newton's work is found in the rural areas of Northumberland, far from public gaze and scrutiny and the admiration and access of more sophisticated city dwellers, has caused his work to suffer by comparison to that of the later architects whose work is concentrated mainly in the city and its immediate environs.

Perhaps, also, as an unashamed admirer of William Newton's lovely buildings this is a fanciful supposition, without foundation, and one verging almost on the paranoia.

Newton was not a prodigious workman, on the scale, for example, of John Dobson. His surviving works number fewer than thirty compared to well over two hundred associated with Dobson. This fact I consider immaterial. His output may well have been much less than Dobson or the Greens but its quality deserves recognition and that is the purpose of this book.

I have simply sought to compile a photographic record (albeit not entirely complete for some of it appears in other of my books) of Newton's architecture: in that aim I feel I have been reasonably successful and have had enormous pleasure in achieving it.

Such a tribute is, I feel, both worthwhile and necessary and it will, hopefully, give my readers the opportunity to judge for themselves whether Newton was, in fact, no more than "a conventional 18th century architect" of limited ability, unworthy to be ranked with Dobson, Wardle et al, or whether he was an underestimated individual who gave pride and pleasure to his employers and a man whose eye for what was 'elegant' was unfailing.

William Newton died n Newcastle, where he had lived all his life, on April 29th, 1798, aged sixty-eight years. He was buried in St Andrew's Church: his tombstone is now covered by the organ.

Number 6, Charlotte Square, was once Newcastle's Royal Grammar School.

In William Newton's list of works, found in "Proceedings of the Society of Antiquaries of Newcastle upon Tyne" (3rd series, volume vi, 1913-14), reference is made to 'a house at the foot of Clayport (Alnwick), occupied successively by the families of Farquar, Dawson and Drysdale'. The date is uncertain. In fact, the house stands on the east side of the Market Place (number 10). It is a tall three-and-a-half storeyed building with sashes and thick architraves to the windows on the first and second floors and little 'Yorkshire sashes' beneath the eaves. The drawing by William Hall, in William Davison's "Descriptive and Historical View of Alnwick" (1822), shows that while the present ground-floor has clearly been altered the west façade of the house, facing into the square, has changed hardly at all over the past one hundred and eighty years.

View from an archway.

The house, standing on the east side of the Market Place, is a tall, three-and-a-half storeyed building with sashes with thick architraves to the windows on the first and second floors and has little "Yorkshire sashes" beneath the eaves. While the present ground-floor has clearly been altered (and is now a coffee house) the west façade of the house, facing into the Square, has changed hardly at all over the past one hundred and eighty years.

Though the house is attributed to William Newton the date is uncertain.

Hesleyside (Bellingham, Northumberland)

For centuries Hesleyside has been associated with the Charlton family. A house and tower were mentioned in 1537, though the old tower, which once stood at the west end of the present building, was probably erected towards the end of the 14th century by Edward Charlton, who held lands in the area, as far back as 1343.

In the 17th century a wing was added and the date 1631 is to be found in a stone over a door in the courtyard.

In 1719 the Hall was re-fronted with a new, south-facing façade: it has heavily segment-headed windows and a parapet.

In the south front ("built as late as 1719, but possibly a century earlier" – Dr Charlton) there is a well-contrived, concealed closet entered by a trap-door, from a passage between two rooms. Air, but not light, seems to have been provided by making the opening behind some old carving, affixed to the wall of the south front.

T R Rowland ("Waters of Tyne") writes, that the entrance to the courtyard is by a central archway (through the south range), and above it "an ornamental shield", set out from the wall, ventilates this secret chamber. The Charlton's were devout Roman Catholics and the first half of the 18th century was troublesome if not dangerous times for those of Catholic persuasion – a secret chamber or 'priest hole' was almost a necessity in any Catholic household with social standing.

In 1738, the Hall was severely damaged by fire. During the subsequent and extensive period of renovation it was struck twice more by damaging fires and, apparently, this damage was not properly repaired until 1796, when the services of William Newton were called upon.

The kitchen and offices were enlarged and altered at a cost of £692. The old walls, damaged by fire, were taken down to ground level and the present east wing was built of hewn ashlar.

The accommodation included a great staircase, hall, dining and drawing rooms, attics and cellars: the work was to cost £1,912 and included polished stone-floors and mahogany woodwork, but not, apparently, plaster work.

Newton rebuilt the old south front adding an extra two right bays, identical in style to the seven already there, also two-and-a-half storeys the south front now has nine bays.

At that time (1796) however, he was actually concentrating his energies rebuilding the east range – an impressive seven-bay, two-and-a-half storeys façade with three-bay pediment. The doorway has Ionic pilasters with a pedimented window above.

The main entrance is now on the north side of the house and has to the left of it a porch of 1796, moved from the east front in the mid-19th century to its present whereabouts.

Around the year 1847 Ignatius Bonomi (c.1787-1870), a friend and distant relative of the Charlton family, carried out alterations to the house including the addition of the clock-tower.

The grounds were laid out by Capability Brown in 1776; his original plans are kept at the house.

The south front (left) and the east front (right) – an impressive seven-bay, two-and-a-half storeyed façade with a three-bay pediment.

In 1796 Newton rebuilt the old south front adding an extra two bays to the right-hand end of the façade. These were identical in style to the seven already there: the south front now boasts nine bays.

Photographed by kind permission of Major John Charlton.

Described as a 'courtyard house' the original entry into the courtyard was by way of an archway through the south front.

In 1719 the Hall was re-fronted with a new, south-facing façade – the archway remains 'but has a door and a window of the later 18th century set within it'.

Photographed by kind permission of Major John Charlton.

The east and north sides of the house.

The main entrance is now on the north side of the house.

It has to the left of it a porch of 1796, moved from the east front in the mid-19th century to its present whereabouts.

Around the year 1847 Ignatius Bonomi carried out alterations to the house including the addition of the clock-tower.

Photographed by kind permission of Major John Charlton.

The courtyard contains a number of interesting features: the small Venetian window on the south wall; the three lovely arched windows, the tripartite window at the top of the wall and the alcove containing a statue of the crucified Christ (the Charlton's are a Catholic family) at ground floor, all on the east wall.

Photographed by kind permission of Major John Charlton.

Capheaton Hall (Northumberland)

Described as "one of the most interesting houses in Northumberland" it is said to be Robert Trollope's... 'most successful design'.

The decoration is flamboyant and original like all Trollope's work. The House was built for Sir John Swinburne: the foundation stone was laid in March 1668 and the mason was Amos Brown. The carpenter was John Potts and the beautiful rustic stone carving around the windows the work of Allen Johnson.

The interior decoration, we know, was the work of a London painter, one Robert Crossby: the architect, of course, was Robert Trollope.

Claims by other writers and commentators, including papers held in the Northumberland County Records Office; the magazine Country Life (edition of August 12th, 1965); Nikolaus Pevsner, Frank Graham, Lyall Wilkes, etc, that William Newton rebuilt the north front in 1789-90, are strenuously dismissed by the present owner, John Browne-Swinburne, who is convinced there is irrefutable proof that while Newton supervised the actual building work the plans for the north front were, in fact, drawn up by one John Tasker. The north front was extended and refaced at the end of the 18th century in what Graham calls "a dull, classical style" but what Pevsner describes as "very plain but really quite grand".

Lyall Wilkes also describes it as a "correct if somewhat dull classical façade (built) at the then rear of the house" and he goes on to complain that it obliterates Trollope's great pilasters and stone carving "to accord with the then less than exuberant taste of the gentry".

The north façade was converted into the front, main entrance of the house instead of the rear – which was its original function.

It has seven bays with a three-bay pedimented centre and lower 'L-plan' projecting wings. The porch has two Tuscan columns.

The main south front has five bays and is two storeys high with four giant pilasters, which are flatly rusticated at the bottom, with banded intermittent rustication higher up and with "thick, bulgy, rock-like rustication" at the first floor level.

The pilasters have no capitals and no connection with the cornice.

The door-case has columns carved with vine leaves. The plinths are decorated with the figures of a knight and a beggar.

The 'curly' open pediment above the door, so popular in Northumberland, is typical late 17th century.

The tall windows are divided by stone mullions not the more usual mullion and transom crosses. The windows are framed with stone bands beautifully decorated with garlands. Two of the windows are carved vases with flowers above them and two have sundials, with dry-tooth ornament around them.

The west side is similar but only has three bays.

There is a fine doorway on the east side of the house.

William Newton also remodelled the interior.

Some of the small rooms with tunnel vaults and charming segmental-vaulted ceilings; the two-roomed library with its plain plaster ceiling and the central staircase, with its glass dome above and strangely plain hand rail… are all Newton's work.

The north front… planned by John Tasker; the building work is believed to have been supervised by William Newton.

Photographed by kind permission of Mr John Browne-Swinburne.

The south front has five bays and is two storeys high. It has four giant pilasters, which are flatly rusticated at the bottom, with banded intermittent rustication higher up and "thick, bulgy, rock-like rustication" at the first floor level.

The pilasters have no capitals and no connection with the cornice.

The tall windows are divided by stone mullions not the more usual mullion and transom crosses.

Two of the windows have carved vases with flowers above them and two have sundials.

Photographed by kind permission of Mr John Browne-Swinburne.

The door-case on the south front has columns beautifully carved with vine leaves. The plinths are decorated with the figures of a knight (left) and a beggar (right). The 'curly' open pediment above the door is typical late 17th century.

The Swinburnes are said to have been resident here since the latter part of the 13th century; Allan de Swinburn having purchased the 'castle' from Sir Thomas de Fenwick in 1274.

In the Civil War the Swinburnes supported the King. As a result the estate, held at that time by William Swinburne, was sequestrated by parliament in 1639. William's grandson John, was created a baronet by Charles II and later married Isabel Lawson, who gave him twenty-four children – 13 daughters and 11 sons. He it was who built the present Hall on a new site, a little to the east of the old fortification, in 1668, having demolished "the faire castle" of his ancestors.

(The Swinburne coat-of-arms.)

The three-bay west front.

A little to the west of the present Hall there formerly stood what has been termed 'a large border stronghold'.

The 'stronghold' is found in the list of castles, fortalices and towers in the County of Northumberland, compiled in 1415.

Listed as "Castrum de Swinburne" but in the margin its status was corrected to that of "Fortalicium" – a fortalice being a small castle or large tower, though as Capheaton had both a moat and a drawbridge perhaps it was a larger than usual 'small castle'.

Photographed by kind permission of Mr John Browne-Swinburne.

The east side of the hall has only three bays but four of the same giant pilasters found on the south front.

It also has a remarkably fine doorway.

Photographed by kind permission of Mr John Browne-Swinburne.

Above the ornamental jamb of the east doorway is a heraldic tablet containing various quarterings of the builder and his ancestors.

Photographed by kind permission of Mr John Browne-Swinburne.

Castle Eden Hall (Castle Eden, County Durham)

The existing house at Castle Eden, was in fact, the remains of a Manor House which had hitherto occupied the site.

The development of Castle Eden dates from a period after 1757 when Rowland Burdon, the elder, a member of the Company of Merchant Adventurers of Newcastle bought the existing house and lands from William Burghley – who had been Secretary of State to Queen Anne.

William Newton began work on the house in 1765 and when he died, in 1798, the major part of the present Castle Eden Hall would have been completed – "though it is unlikely that the detail and external facing design of the house was as Newton designed it".

Castle Eden is Gothic in detail with hood moulded sash windows, embattled with small corner turrets – which were not Newton's style.

Completed in 1786, by 1823 it was described as 'lately rebuilt' – clearly suggesting a hand other than William Newton's.

Rowland Burdon's son, Rowland Burdon the younger, inherited the house and estate on his father's death, in 1786, and there is evidence to suggest (- the younger Burdon's association with both John Soane, a leading architect of his time, and William Atkinson of Bishop Auckland… who designed the Gothic gateway entrance and lodges) that Newton's original building was altered externally, subsequent to the younger Burdon inheriting the estate.

One much later alteration took place in 1893 when the large courtyard to the north of the building (surrounded by a curtain wall and containing stables) was reduced by the insertion of a further wing containing a library and various other rooms.

This extension, we read, was 'built of freestone salvaged from Castle Eden Colliery after the disastrous floods of 1890'.

The south and west façades.

Across the entire length of the west front of the house is a large 'palm house' (entirely prefabricated of concrete blocks), of 1863, built to designs of F R Hicks of Newcastle.

A curious addition since being of reconstructed stone 'it appears oddly dark and dull against the shining Hesledon limestone of the main building'.

Photographed by kind permission of Mr Tony Gillman.

Built in classical form (three-storeyed, seven by five bays), the three central bays on the east façade are canted: Gothicised by the embattled parapet and small corner turrets and the hood moulded (ie imitation Perpendicular) sash windows.

Photographed by kind permission of Mr Tony Gillman.

The rebuilding of the church by William Newton, for Rowland Burdon, began shortly after 1757 and was completed by 1764 – with the addition of a steeple. "St James' is built on the site of a chapel known to have been standing there as far back as 1143: it is an example of early Georgian Gothic style." (Neville Whittaker)

The nave is divided from the aisles by giant Corinthian columns.

The east window is Palladian, 'Venetian' style.

A small late 18th century house 'in the William Newton style'.

The south front of five by four bays has a pedimented Venetian doorway and above it a tripartite sash window, reminiscent of Lemmington Hall. The Hall has a hipped roof and quoins at each corner of the block.

Photographed by kind permission of Mr R W T Thorp.

The south front with the broken pedimented Venetian doorway and tripartite window above it on the first floor.

Photographed by kind permission of Mr R W T Thorp.

The Craster family has lived here since at least the 12th century: Albert Craster, founder of the 'dynasty' was in possession of Craster before 1168 and, as members of the same family are living there today (2005) this means that Albert's descendants have occupied the Tower (and house) for almost nine hundred years.

The present, three-storey, five-bay 'new house' was added to the south side of the Tower, in 1769.

The central doorway is tripartite, with Tuscan pilasters and an open pediment. The second floor window beneath the main pediment has a detached section of cornice above – similar to that on the west front at Shawdon Hall. 'This, and other features, suggests the hand of William Newton'.

Photographed by kind permission of Mr and Mrs J Michael Craster and Miss Mary D Cra'ster.

The three-storey, battlemented tower (the battlements, incidentally, are a fairly modern addition) certainly existed as far back as the beginning of the 15th century (it is mentioned in the County's list of castles, fortalices and towers compiled in 1415).

It has a ten feet high, vaulted basement and a wheel stair in the south-east corner where the wall is almost six and a half feet thick. The adjacent east wing has four feet thick walls which, Pevsner believes, suggests a medieval or 16th century date but this part of the tower was extended and remodelled in the nineteenth century.

The south front, with quoins at both ends, is faced with square whinstone and it has a central, open pediment.

The central doorway is tripartite, with Tuscan pilasters and it, too, is surmounted by an open pediment.

Many of the house's characteristics suggest the hand of William Newton – the floating cornice above the central, second-floor window, for example, is also a feature at Shawdon Hall (near Glanton), which many believe is also the work of William Newton.

Photographed by kind permission of Mr and Mrs J Michael Craster and Miss Mary D Cra'ster.

Dissington Hall (Dalton, Northumberland)

Dissington Hall has been described as "one of the finest Georgian mansions in Northumberland".

Although not actually built until 1797 the impressive Grade II* listed building has retained almost all of the architectural features shown in the original building plans drawn up by local Newcastle architect, William Newton, in 1794.

Stewart Bonney, editor of "the Northumbrian", writing in the December 2000/January 2001 edition of that estimable magazine, suggests it is quite possible Newton never actually saw the finished building for (Bonney writes) "when his original drawings came to light in the 1970s they were marked 'never built'".

The house was built for Edward Collingwood, cousin of the celebrated Admiral, Lord Cuthbert Collingwood – Nelson's second-in-command never actually lived at Dissington preferring instead his compact and more modest quarters at Chirton Hall (or House, as it is sometimes called).

* The village of Chirton was situated a mile or so west of North Shields.

Built at the end of the 17th century Edward Collingwood had lived at Chirton Hall from the end of the 18th century (when he inherited the house from his father, Edward Snr) until his demise in 1806, when the property, it is said, passed to his cousin, the famous Admiral. The Admiral never lived at Chirton, however, spending most of his life at sea apart from his very rare visits to his house in Oldgate, Morpeth.

Apparently his wife and daughters *did* spend some time at Chirton. Another account tells that prior to his death Edward wisely ensured that his entire estate at Dissington should remain in the hands of his family by offering it to a great-nephew, one Edward Spenser-Stanhope, on condition that he change his name by deed poll (a by no means unusual practice among the landed gentry when valuable property was at stake) – to Collingwood. Not surprisingly the young man agreed with alacrity to his uncle's proposal although it was 1817 before he eventually inherited the property.

NCRO documents show that in the 1820s Edward made commendable improvements to both the estate and the Hall including the addition of the two-storey east wing and a formal entrance porch (both shown in Newton's original plans) and a stable-block.

Edward and his wife, Arabella, unfortunately produced no male heir and so their son-in-law, as Edward himself had done, adopted the Collingwood family name – thus ensuring the succession.

Although the Hall remained a possession of the Collingwood's until c.1950, when they sold the Dissington estate to the Church Commissioners, from the beginning of the 20th century the family chose to live on one of their other estates. Two of their tenants who subsequently occupied the hall were Emmerson Bainbridge (founder of the Newcastle department store) and James Deuchar (of the well-known brewing family), who installed servants' bell-pulls everywhere and was also the proud owner of two pink, Rolls-Royce motor cars.

In 1939, the house was requisitioned for use both as a military hospital and a billet for W.A.A.F.s stationed at nearby Ouston.

The nine-bay south front. The centre of the façade is a full-height, canted, three-bay window, behind which, on the ground floor, is an octagonal-shaped room. The building is two-and-a-half storeys.

The original building plans were drawn up by Newcastle architect, William Newton, in 1794 and the house was built for Edward Collingwood (cousin of the famous Admiral) in 1797.

The house remained in the possession of the Collingwood family until 1950 when the estate was sold to the Church Commissioners who still retain ownership of much of the surrounding farmland.

Photographed by kind permission of Mr Michael Brown.

The Browns arrived in 1968 when Michael, the present owner, 'was but a lad' and for many of the years since Michael and his family have carried on a relentless programme of restoration and repair unselfishly devoting their financial resources to this worthy end and striving throughout for accuracy and authenticity.

The success of their business venture (the Hall is now a popular venue for wedding receptions) coupled with a ready access to Newton's plans and designs, have together ensured that Dissington (as Michael has so colourfully and proudly described it) is now "keeping ahead of the forces of Nature".

Photographed by kind permission of Michael Brown.

Described as ‘a grand old house of c.1781, for Robert Lisle – attributed to William Newton’.

The design is very similar to Shawdon Hall, which has also been attributed to Newton.

Two-storeyed, it has a seven-bay ashlar front with a three-bay centrepiece, with giant, Ionic pilasters, a fluted frieze and pediment. A flight of stone steps up to the central doorway which is of the Venetian type, favoured by Robert Adam, and is a feature at both Shawdon and Backworth Hall – both attributed to William Newton.

Photographed by kind permission of Mr and Mrs D Moore.

Shawdon Hall is said to be one of the finest classical houses in Northumberland. Built in 1779 for William Hargrave, on the site of an old pele tower: the tower is mentioned in 1403 and must have been a place of importance as it was called a 'castrum' in 1415, and was 'in measurable good reparacions' in 1541 there is little doubt that the 'castrum' stood in the grounds of the present Hall.

The two-storeyed, seven-bay, south front has a three-bay centre with steps leading up to a lovely Venetian doorway. The decorated central pediment is supported by four giant pilasters and contains an 1817 wood-carving of the Pawson coat-of-arms.

The architect of Shawdon Hall is unknown but on stylistic grounds the balance of probability is that it is likely to have been the work of William Newton of Newcastle.

Photographed by kind permission of Major R F H Cowen.

The west front has five bays with a central open pediment and a floating cornice over the first floor window beneath: there is another pediment over a wing set back to the left.

Photographed by kind permission of Major R F H Cowen.

The medieval 'Turris de Howicke' was included in the survey of 1415. In 1538, it was described as 'a little pile, a mile from the shore'.

This old, medieval tower was pulled down c.1780 to make way for the present Hall, built for Earl Grey in 1782, from designs by William Newton.

The south front is nine bays wide with a projected, three-bay, pedimented centre. The ground floor is rusticated: the upper floors of the centrepiece have four giant, unfluted Ionic columns.

The present owner (Lord Howick of Glendale) and his family live in Newton's west pavilion: the east pavilion is used as a stable block. The main block of the Hall (featured) is occupied by offices.

Photographed by kind permission of Lord Howick.

The south front is nine bays wide with a projected, three-bay, pedimented centre. The ground floor is rusticated: the upper floors of the centrepiece have four giant, unfluted Ionic columns.

Photographed by kind permission of Lord Howick.

The five-bay east front: again, the ground floor is rusticated.

Photographed by kind permission of Lord Howick.

In 1809 the main entrance to the Hall was transferred from the south side to the north and "a Tuscan, one-storey addition was made there to receive the entrance hall".

Above the entrance two giant, Tuscan columns flanked by circular and shoulder-headed windows lie beneath a carved pediment.

Photographed by kind permission of Lord Howick.

Designed by William Newton and built between 1772-75 for Lord Percy, in the castellated style, as 'a house for moor-game shooting' (ie a hunting lodge).

It is quadrangular in shape with an arched entrance.

The original, symmetrical, north front with the central arched entrance.

The north front.

Photographed by kind permission of the Forestry Commission:
(J G S Gill, Forest District Manager)

The history of Lemmington began some eight hundred years ago with one Siward de Lemmington, but it was probably a member of the Beadnell family who built the pele tower, sometime in the 14th century. The Beadnells occupied the pele during the next four centuries until it passed into the hands of the Claverings. Eventually, the tower passed into the possession of the redoubtable Fenwicks, through marriage, and it was during their occupancy that the splendid Georgian house, adjoining the Tower, was built, in 1746. The Hall remained the property of the Fenwicks until it was purchased by William Pawson, at the end of the 19th century. The south front has nine bays. The projecting centre bay has a beautiful Venetian doorway under a tripartite window and a pediment.

The two ground-floor bay-windows, either side of the main entrance, are also pedimented. By the end of the 19th century this lovely, mid-18th century country house, altered towards the end of that century by William Newton, had become a roofless ruin.

Photographed by kind permission of Sir Charles Aitchison Bart.

The pele tower is a typically 14th century, L shaped construction. Measuring fifty-three feet by thirty-five feet, it is slightly greater in size than the equally imposing tower at Chipchase, which 'only' measures fifty-one and a half feet by thirty-four feet.

The walls of the pele tower are said to be some six and a half feet thick.

Photographed by kind permission of Sir Charles Aitchison Bart.

The medieval Church of St Bartholomew was repaired and rebuilt by William Newton, in 1790. The church is said to be of particular interest because of its early Gothic revival, square west tower, with pointed belfry openings, pinnacled battlements and short, octagonal spire. Indeed, the church has been rather flatteringly described as 'a well-proportioned composition of 1790'.

There has been a church on this site since medieval times.

The present church, designed by William Newton, and built for the Newcastle Corporation (1764-8) as a chapel-of-ease for David Stephenson's All Saints' Church, at the bottom of Pilgrim Street, was consecrated in 1768.

The church was built largely using stone from the old city wall and its churchyard contains the graves of many who died in the late great cholera epidemic to hit the city.

Described as "a stately classical church in sandstone ashlar... with a plain and well-designed west tower".

The Assembly Rooms (Fenkle Street, Newcastle upon Tyne)

Planned by William Newton and built between 1774-6, in what was then the grounds of St John's Church, a special Act of Parliament was needed before the work could begin, as the Vicar of St John's held the lease.

Described by David Lovey as "a splendid, neo-classical, symmetrical building with Greek columns, handsome but simple windows and tasteful lower wings". The building cost £6,700.

The Assembly Rooms became a focal point for public meetings, debates; grand, colourful balls as well as select, private parties.

Fashionable cities like York and Bath already had Assembly rooms – York's (of 1732) are described as "somewhat less refined and elegant"; Bath's (of 1771) as "comparable in scale and quality", but, whereas Bath's had to be restored, having been severely damaged during World War II, Newcastle's are substantially original and were the first to be built in any industrial city anywhere in England.

The building comprises a brick body with polished stone façade: the canopy or portico over the main entrance is an unfortunate 20th century addition. Newton's design, both inside and out, is supremely elegant: all its features reflect its neo-classical taste – "the subtly articulated flatness of the façade: the windows of the low wings, set in semi-circular arches and the paired columns at either end of the central block".

The capitals of the six, Ionic columns are of special interest, being particularly un-Palladian in type: they derive from the Ionic order of the Erechtheion, on the Acropolis.

The interior, especially of the ballroom with its seven, magnificent chandeliers (one of which is said to have cost six hundred guineas), and the fine plaster work, is "a superb example of provincial, decorative design, completely in the Adam manner".

The pilasters, for example, "have lost all pretence of a functional role and are merely vehicles for decoration".

"The Tyneside Classical Tradition", describe it as "… certainly the finest, non-domestic interior in the region".

There were also cardrooms, a library, newsroom, a coffee room and a huge, supper room.

The Assembly Rooms (Fenkle Street, Newcastle upon Tyne)

The Assembly Rooms, designed by William Newton and opened in 1776, were said to be "the most elegant and commodious edifice of the kind in the kingdom, except the House of Assembly in Bath".

The north-front, by William Newton (c.1800-05) is two-storeyed; eleven bays wide with giant Tuscan columns and it, too, has a pediment. It is built of red brick with stone dressings.

The Hall (now St Mary's College) is now part of the University of Newcastle and provides accommodation for some 370 students.

Photographed by kind permission of the University of Newcastle (Registrar's office: M J Warwicker, Head of Press and Communications).

South front.

The projecting three-bay centre. All the windows are recessed with architraves. The whole is surmounted by a decorated pediment.

Photographed by kind permission of the University of Newcastle (Registrar's office: M J Warwicker, Head of Press and Communications).

The east front is of mid-nineteenth century construction.

Italianate: two-storeyed and nine bays wide. The projecting wings are each of two bays; the recessed centre is of five bays.

A flight of stone steps leads up to an interesting doorway.

In 1835 William Ord sold the Hall.

The west front was added to in 1906, by Leonard Stokes.

On the south side of the Sandhill is the Guildhall, the ancient centre of civic government. It was originally designed, in 1658, by Robert Trollope, but the building we see today bears little resemblance to his 17th century construction.

David Stephenson and William Newton redesigned the north face (featured) between 1794-6. The design of the projecting centre, of five bays with the three centre bays separated by four beautiful Ionic columns, is very similar in appearance to Newton's Assembly Rooms, on Fenkle Street.

Newton Hall is a late 18th century house, built for John Forster and probably designed by William Newton. The five-bay south front is almost identical to Togston Hall (also believed to be the work of Newton) except it is raised on a low basement. Built of lovely pink, sandstone ashlar the three centre bays are capped by an open pediment the apex of which is crowned with a marble statue: a leafy urn stands above each bottom corner of the pediment. The main entrance has a flight of twelve stone steps flanked by wrought iron balustrades. Set back from the building, on the west side, there is a gable end of a stone-block containing a blind Venetian window under a large round arch.

The canted bay which is the central feature of the five-bay east front.

Photographed by kind permission of Mr J I Patterson.

Togston Hall (North Togston, near Amble, Northumberland)

Though not in the list of fortalices, towers and castles, in the county, composed for Henry V, in 1415 (no mention is made of any tower at Togston), there seems to have been some kind of small stronghold there – a bastle, perhaps, with thick walls and slit windows.

It stood on a site a little to the north-west of Mr Lawson-Smith's house until around 1820 when it was taken down by Mr T G Smith… "to his subsequent and lasting regret".

The family of Smith held lands in Amble in, and probably before, the reign of Queen Elizabeth I.

William Smith, who purchased lands in Togston, after 1639 and before 1658, acquired other lands there, through his marriage with one of John Patterson's daughters.

His son made additions to the house, already 140 years old, and above what was (probably) the south, outer-door caused the following letters and figures to be cut in relief – "16 TFS 85": a sundial in the garden bears the initials of his grandson – "17 TS (B?) 45".

The house was remodelled in that year (1685) with the addition of a rear stair-wing.

In the late 18th century the house was enlarged and the old building became only the rear premises to a new, five-bay, front block of ashlar with sill-bands and an open pediment above a central, projecting bay.

The design of the present building has many similarities to Newton Hall (at Newton-by-the-Sea) and the architect at Togston was very likely to have been William Newton.

The fine... trees, which now shelter the house and gardens, were probably planted at that time.

The 'modern' house, with its five-bay, south front and sill bands. The central bay is topped with an open pediment. The main, south entrance is flanked by columns surmounted, also, with an open pediment.

The building has a hipped roof.

The old house became only the rear premises after Newton's alterations.

Togston Hall (North Togston, near Amble, Northumberland)

In the late 18th century the old house was enlarged and a new ashlar front was added: the architect is very likely to have been William Newton of Newcastle.

Photographed by kind permission of Mr Robert Gelley.

There are still traces of a 9th century Anglian church to be seen here (- remains of an Anglian stone cross, part of a tomb, etc) but St Mungo's is, essentially a 13th century building – though, despite its appearance, little survives even from that period. "Its several restorations have happily, almost miraculously, preserved its character down the ages". Its decorative style is typically Victorian. It is an attractive church of dark grey stone with a number of interesting features, not least the four-bay nave, its bell-cote at the west end, the north porch and long chancel (-at fifty-one feet the chancel is only eleven feet shorter than the nave). The aisle walls were rebuilt and a transeptal chapel removed by Robert and William Newton, in 1772. The chancel was rebuilt by Anthony Salvin, in 1863-4, and further restoration work was carried out by R J Johnson, between 1875-7.

The west wall, three-and-a-half feet thick, is of 13th century construction – except for the large 'modern' window, inserted in imitation of the 'five sisters' window in York Minster.

The present, open-timbered roof was put in during the restoration of 1877: the stone interior of the church, which had been plastered, was stripped and the aisle windows replaced by windows of Early English pattern. The north porch was added and the chancel arch rebuilt – all the work of R J Johnson.

View through the 13th century style lynch-gate.

The ‘long chancel’. The chancel arch dates back to the thirteenth century but the chancel itself was rebuilt, in 1863-4, by Anthony Salvin.

The fine, 13th century piscina, with a moulded, trefoiled arch, is one of the few double piscinas in existence, having two sinks, very rare but typical of some in the 13th century. After seven and a half centuries it is still used regularly at Holy Communion.

Towards the west end of the chancel there is a low-side 'leper window'. The glass shows four angels playing unusual musical instruments.

Whitfield Hall (Whitfield, near Hexham, Northumberland)

Whitfield Hall has breathtaking views overlooking the river West Allen. Originally it was a fortalice built in the time of Henry VI – remains of the medieval tower are said to be incorporated in the rear wing but, as Pevsner explains, "there is very little stonework left… to mark the site of the fortalices".

The original hall, built in the 17th century, was a large, square, stone building and was an addition to the old medieval fortress.

In the middle of the 18th century the Whitfield family found themselves in serious financial difficulties and were obliged to sell their estate to William Ord who, at the time was living at Fenham Hall, just outside of Newcastle.

William Ord rebuilt the house, in 1785, from plans by William Newton, at a cost of something in excess of £17,000.

Newton's house, as illustrated in a painting by E Swinburne, c.1840, shows an elegant building with a five-bay south front and a three-bay pedimented centre: the tall, ground-floor windows either side of the arched doorway are also pedimented. The house was two-storeyed and Georgian in style.

Its appearance was drastically altered, however, as a result of the alterations that took place in 1856 when, amongst other 'enhancements' a second storey was added and all the windows altered.

"The current appearance of the Hall," writes the present owner, "is (sadly) not at all as William Newton intended".

"It is a shame," he goes on, "that the Victorians never seemed to have enough room to fit in servants and furniture as I don't think the alterations were, in fact, 'improvements'".

Further alterations were made in 1968 and in 1976 the house was damaged by fire.

The second storey and balustrade were added in 1856 and all the windows were altered.

Photographed by kind permission of Mr John Blackett-Ord.

Whitfield Hall (Whitfield, near Hexham, Northumberland)

The canted bay, which is the prominent feature of the east front, stands left of centre of the seven-bay façade; there being three bays to its right while only one on the left.

Photographed by kind permission of Mr John Blackett-Ord.

The entire east façade.

The stonework on the east front of the Hall, with its hipped roof, balustrade and quoined window frames, is clearly the older part of the house.

Photographed by kind permission of Mr John Blackett-Ord.

The balustraded four-bay west front with single-projecting centre.

Photographed by kind permission of Mr John Blackett-Ord.

The site has been occupied since the 13th century. The land in medieval times belonged to the Turpin family, then the Reads and then to the Bewickes. The Bewickes were merchant adventurers of Newcastle and in 1779 they built this fine Hall on the site of the Close House Chantry, demolished to make way for the present Hall. The architect is unrecorded but it is likely to have been William Newton.

The style is classical. The south front (featured) has two-and-a-half storeys and five-bays. It has a slight three-bay projection with pediment.

The doorway has Ionic columns to support the doorhead.

The east front.

The east and west fronts are likewise two-and-a-half storeys with five bays. The projecting bay, to the right, is a later addition.

There is a conservatory of five bays, with Tuscan columns, to the north-west.

Photographed by kind permission of the University of Newcastle (Registrar's Office: M J Warwicker, Head of Press & Communications).

Obituary:

The report of Newton's death in the Newcastle Advertiser of Saturday May 5th, 1798, reads:-

Died

On Sunday, 29th April, after a long and painful illness at his house in Charlotte Square, in the town, Mr William Newton, architect, in the 69th year of his age.

As a man his integrity, sobriety and diligence procured him many valuable friends and as an architect his memory will be perpetuated in the various edifices planned and built by him in this town and in the counties adjacent.

The Annual Report (March, 1799) of Newcastle's Literary and Philosophical Society records:-

'During the last year the Society has been deprived by the death of… Mr William Newton, a very worthy and amiable man whose abilities as an architect will be acknowledged so long as Castle Eden, Howick and the Assembly Rooms in this town shall remain'.

The obituary printed in the Newcastle (Weekly) Chronicle of Saturday May 5th, 1798, was exactly the same as that found in the Newcastle Adviser. Sadly, the Newcastle Courant made no reference to Newton's passing and, for some reason, the Daily Journal was not printed at all in 1798 so that only two of the city's journals carried the news of his death.

Newton's solitary obituary is both brief and muted – especially when it is contrasted to those written of Newcastle's more celebrated architect, John Dobson, on the occasion of his demise in 1865 and whose notices were more numerous, colourful and fulsome.

References are made in the Advertiser to Newton's character – a man of integrity, sobriety and diligence: others refer to him as a worthy and amiable man: but admirable though these qualities are (and any man would be pleased and flattered to have them inscribed on his epitaph) the fact remains they might so easily apply to thousands of his fellow citizens who had also led largely blameless if rather undistinguished lives.

The newspapers also refers, vaguely, to "various edifices" planned and built by Newton yet singularly fails to mention even one by name – no acknowledgement of Fenham Hall, his lovely Church of St Ann on City Road: no mention of his work at Howick Hall, Backworth, Hesleyside, Dissington or Whitfield or any of the other surviving monuments of his talents as an architect.

True, the report of the Literary and Philosophical Society alludes to three of his works – yet he was associated with almost thirty!

Surely the man who designed the city's Assembly Rooms (described as "a splendid neo-classical building… comparable in scale and quality to those in Bath") deserved rather more than the scant, subdued and somewhat bland eulogy accorded him.

Comparisons are said to be odious and if not odious often grossly unfair. John Dobson, for example, was associated with more than two hundred ventures here in the North East of England. Newton cannot be compared to Dobson either in terms of quality or output and one would not wish to suggest otherwise. History has been much kinder to Dobson.

Following his death on the 8th of January, 1865 the Newcastle Daily Journal (of January 16th) recorded almost all of Dobson's works: perhaps it was William Newton's destiny to die as he had lived – honest and reliable but unremarkable!

Part Three

John and Benjamin Green

Profile

John Green (1787-1852) was born on June 20th, 1787, at Newton Fell House, Nafferton – two miles, or so, north of Ovington, in Northumberland. John's father, Benjamin Senior, was a carpenter and manufacturer of agricultural implements.

When John 'came of age' he joined his father in the business and as it expanded and grew (due in no small part to John's energy and enterprise) they moved their workshop to Corbridge, a market town, on the banks of the Tyne, some three miles from Hexham.

John and his father extended their activities to general building work. John turned his attention to the architectural side of the business and c.1820 he left Corbridge for Newcastle where he thereafter practised as an architect and civil engineer.

John Green had two sons; John Junior (c.1807-68) and Benjamin (c.1811-58), named after his grandfather, both of whom became successful architects – though sadly and perhaps inexplicably, John Junior seems to have disappeared from the pages of history without trace or further reference: the "John and Benjamin Green" partnership so frequently referred to in the annals of north-east architecture, in the nineteenth century, is, in fact, that of father and son and definitely *not* the two brothers.

John Green has been described as a 'plain, practical, shrewd man of business': his son as 'an artistic, dashing sort of fellow' whose style was 'ornamental, florid and costly' while his father's was plain, severe and economical': thus, their partnership appears superficially, at least, to have been based, in part, on an attraction of opposites.

Opinions of their talents seem to vary somewhat to extremes but that they had several 'strings to their bow' seems beyond doubt.

They were particularly active as railway architects and they enjoyed something of a reputation for designing farmhouses: they designed and altered churches, fine houses and public buildings: the senior partner specialised in the erection of bridges.

John Grundy and Grace McCombie, writing in Pevsner's excellent 1992 edition of "The Buildings of England: Northumberland", have this to say:-

"John and Benjamin Green (designed) several simple little churches with nave, chancel and bellcote; true, in a sense, to the commonest medieval type in the country, but *uninspiring in imitation*, eg Dalton (1836), the Church of the Holy Trinity and the Holy Saviour Church (1836-7) at Sugley. Their most impressive churches are Earsdon (1836-7) and Cambo (1842) – but the best of the Early English churches are by John Dobson".

“Between them”, writes H Colvin, in his ‘A Biographical Dictionary of British Architects: 1600-1840’, “they designed a number of Gothic churches *of no special distinction*, and ruthlessly altered some old ones, in a manner which showed *they were no antiquarians*”.

Richard Welford, in “Men of Mark Twixt Tyne and Tweed” (1895), rates them highly:-

“Mr Dobson may fairly be styled the father of the architectural profession, in Newcastle, as he was the first President of the Architects’ Association: the Greens (of the Arcade) ranked next to Mr Dobson”. High praise, indeed! In a letter to the editor of the Newcastle Weekly News (January 7th, 1887), one Percy L Addison, of Gillhead, Moresby, Whitehaven, also declares his admiration:-

“I believe the North of England has rarely produced men who combined, like the Greens, refined, architectural taste with great engineering skill. Care and refinement can be traced in every line of their work. They lived at a time when artistic taste was dormant, or only waking and yet their works may stand as a lesson to many in the present day who, through the advance of taste, have enjoyed greater advantages”.

Not everything shared Mr Addison’s unequivocal approval, however. For while the Greens certainly enjoyed their successes and deserve full credit for these their reputation was not entirely unblemished and it would be folly to ignore their failures.

The Church of St Bartholomew, in Whittingham, Northumberland, remains a monument to their less than triumphant endeavours.

In 1839-40 they pulled down the beautiful and rather unique 8th century Saxon tower to rebuild it “bigger and better” in the nineteenth century Gothic style.

At the same time they ruthlessly and pointlessly removed the 12th century Norman arches, forming an arcade on the north aisle and for some incomprehensible reason substituted imitation arches in their stead.

W W Tomlinson, in his “Comprehensive Guide to Northumberland”, describes the ‘restoration’ work as *“disastrous”*. The 1992 edition of Pevsner’s “The Buildings of England: Northumberland”, condemns the Greens’ work as *“vandalism”*.

These two can hardly be described as unqualified enthusiasts for or supporters of the Greens’ architectural abilities.

In 1827 one of the pinnacles of the St Nicholas’ Church (later the Cathedral) was observed to totter when the bells were rung. On subsequent examination a number of serious faults were found and steps were proposed to rectify these in order to make the steeple safe.

The work progressed slowly while the Corporation and Churchwardens wrangled over liability. Scaffolding erected in 1827 was still in place two years later. The situation and the state of the tower continued to deteriorate alarmingly.

Finally, in 1832 (a full five years after the initial examination had revealed the extent of the problem) reports were obtained from both John Green and John Dobson (Green's perhaps more celebrated contemporary – both men were born in the same year); both of whom declared their detailed proposals. Ultimately and after much discussion it was agreed that Dobson should be the Corporation's architect and that he should preserve the tower at the joint expense of both church and town but that Green's scheme should also be adopted 'to satisfy the public clamour for visible buttresses' but that he should proceed solely at the expense of the church.

It would appear, however, that the Greens' involvement went far beyond 'visible buttresses' and a list of their other work is catalogued in volume ix of the 1932 edition of 'Archaeologia Aeliana'.

"Doubtless in time", writes H L Honeyman, rather sarcastically, "they would have rebuilt the whole church, but death removed John Green in 1852 and his son (Benjamin) in 1858".

'Most of the Green's work in the church … was bolder and coarser, in detail, than John Dobson's and their share of the work in St Nicholas' is no exception.'

An article in the edition of the Newcastle Weekly Chronicle (January 1st, 1887), Supplement, is highly critical of another piece of John Green's work: his designs for a new front for the Scots Church on Blackett Street, Newcastle. "Mr John Green had designed, for the Corporation, a new front to the Blackett Street, Scotch Church. The front projected angularly into the line of Blackett Street and required to be set back. Unfortunately, the style chosen was 'tabernacle Gothic', which was then adopted by joiners for garden and other cheap extensions. This front appeared in Welby Pugin's "Contrasts" and was at once recognised as an example of the bad taste of the period."

In that same article the correspondent writes both sneeringly and patronisingly (and many might suggest a little unfairly) of Benjamin Green's railway stations - " …..they may now be inconvenient (?) as stations but they are, at least, picturesque and when the flowers and trees about them appear in full bloom they look like charming little villas."

In the following week's edition of that same newspaper, Percy Addison of Whitehaven leaps to the Green's defence, complaining bitterly that the article featured so prominently the previous week had "… omitted to mention some of the Green's best works selecting for criticism some of those which had no artistic merit".

He adds: "… the article is likely to mislead and give the readers anything but a true impression of the works of those gentlemen".

Opinions on the merits and weaknesses of these two architects, as I have already pointed out, are diverse and divided – this was so a hundred years ago and nothing much has changed over the passing century.

If I reserve the right to 'sit, unashamedly, on the proverbial fence' it is because I feel it is politic to do so. Without the essential qualifications needed to make an informed judgement of the quality of the Greens' work it would be presumptuous of me to abandon my position of impartiality.

Moreover, the object of this book is, as far as possible, simply to photograph their surviving work in the County of Northumberland and the City of Newcastle without making any personal criticism: I have left that to others.

I have recorded comments and statements made by those whose opinions are far more worthy of note than any of mine would be simply for the purpose of demonstrating to the reader that, if nothing else, the work of John and Benjamin Green certainly provoked controversy.

Under John Green's supervision work commenced on Cresswell Hall, in Northumberland, in 1821. Frank Graham, in "The Old Halls, Houses and Inns of Northumberland", writes. 'The designs were by London architect, John Shaw and the work was carried out under the supervision of *Benjamin Green of Newcastle'.

* Here Graham is in error, for in 1821 Benjamin Green was only ten years old! The statement should, of course, attribute the work to John Green.

In 1822, he began the building of the Newcastle headquarters of the Literary and Philosophical Society, on Westgate Road. An inscribed silver trowel was presented to Green by the Duke of Sussex on the occasion of the laying of the foundation stone.

His next work of real significance was the Scotswood Suspension Bridge – alas, no more!

It was begun on the 21st of July, 1830 and eventually opened on April 12th, 1931, when John Green was presented with a silver claret jug as a memento of the occasion, on which was engraved a picture of the bridge.

"Until the construction of Newcastle's High Level Bridge, ten years later," we are told, "the Scotswood Suspension Bridge was 'one of the sights of the district'."

In fact, John Green had actually prepared the *first* design for the High Level Bridge but as the scheme was then adopted by the York, Newcastle and Berwick Railway Company it was decided to award the final design to their own engineer – Robert Stephenson.

Meanwhile, while work was progressing on the bridge at Scotswood John Green undertook other important public works: the foundation stone for the Church of the Holy Trinity, in Usworth,

County Durham, was laid in June, 1831. He also designed a chain bridge, over the river Tees, at Whorlton, three miles south of Barnard Castle, County Durham. Next, he erected a stone bridge across the Tees at Blackwell Ford, Darlington, and after his temporary partnership with John Dobson, securing the foundations of the tower of St Nicholas' Church, in Newcastle, he constructed a bridge over the river Tyne, at Bellingham, in Northumberland, in 1834.

It was about this time (mid-1830s) that young Benjamin Green joined his father in the family business and thenceforth "it became difficult to distinguish the work of the father from that of the son".

Benjamin, at one time, had been a pupil of Augustus Charles Pugin, the elder (1769 – 182?). Pugin had come to Britain as a penniless, non-English speaking, French refugee, at the time of the Revolution in France (1789). At that time Pugin had only a modicum of ability as a draughtsman but, eventually, under the patronage and with the help and encouragement of architect John Nash, he aspired to become one of the best architectural draughtsman of his day.

As a general rule, though by no means exclusively, John Green superintended bridges and engineering work while his son planned public buildings, churches and villas.

In any event, they had now extended the sphere of their operations moving on from "the construction of stables, cowbyres and cottages" to the "erection of country houses and public buildings".

"They did their work well", it is said, "and reaped the reward of well-doing: public confidence."

The chapels-of-ease at Dalton and Sugley, near Newburn, were, in all probability, designed by Benjamin Green.

The Theatre Royal (1836-7), Newcastle, was certainly his conception and the beautiful column supporting the statue of Earl ('Reform Bill') Grey (1838) was almost certainly his, also.

It has already been said that the Greens were particularly active as railway architects. As the extension of the railways gradually became the occupation of architects and engineers, in the North-East of England, the Greens, too, became increasingly involved in this kind of work.

In 1846, George Hudson, the 'Railway King', commissioned Benjamin to design all the railways stations between Newcastle and Berwick.

Fine, handsome buildings, some of them were more like villas built by gentlemen of substance than residences for railway employees. Benjamin planned the booking offices and houses for the stationmasters: his father designed some of the bridges over which the railways ran.

But notwithstanding this remarkable 'vote of confidence' shown by Hudson in the competence of the younger Green the achievement which gave the partnership its predominant reputation was one of John Green's greatest successes. The elder Green, we know, specialised in the erection of bridges and in 1841 he was awarded the Telford Medal of the Institution of Civil Engineers for a system of laminated timber arches with which he had experimented as early as 1827 and which he later employed successfully in his Willington and Ouseburn Bridges, in 1837 – though Willington was later rebuilt in iron in 1867, and the Ouseburn Viaduct was replaced in 1868.

In essence, Green had invented a new method of building wooden bridges for railway transport "across still waters and over deep valleys", considered in their time to be "the highest combination of strength and economy known in railway engineering."

His invention consisted of bending three inch planks of wood, "laminated timber" as it was called, into arches; strengthening them with struts and braces and resting them upon iron plates, or shoes, fixed to stone piers. Green's viaducts, it was said, attracted as much attention, in 1838-9, as did the Forth Bridge, north of Edinburgh, fifty years later.

All John Green's wooden, laminated bridges have now been replaced but his wrought-iron suspension bridge at Whorley still stands as the oldest bridge of its type in the entire country; still supported, unaided, by its original chains.

For several years John Green also held the appointment as "architect of farms, etc," for the Duke of Northumberland, "upon whose estates he erected many good and substantial houses".

John Green died on the 30th of September, 1852, at Newcastle. His son, Benjamin, died, in a mental home in Dinsdale Park, on the 14th of November, 1858 – at the age of only 47.

The Railway Station Master's House (Acklington, Northumberland)

The Station Master's House is now a private residence.

The station itself, was designed by Benjamin Green, in 1847, for the Newcastle and Berwick Railway Company, in his usual Tudor style.

Photographed by kind permission of Mr and Mrs D Charnock.

Built in 1836, from designs by John Green, in the lancet style; there is a narrow gable to the street with trefoil loops flanking the door. There are lancets flanking a two-light window above. At the top of the south-facing gable there is a window shaped like a four-pointed star, flanked by little blind lancets. St Mary's is no longer a place of worship. Work began, in January 2001, to convert the church into a museum – which it now is… the Alnwick and District Museum. Displays feature three principal themes – the moorland and the town; Alnwick's trading history and links with the sea.

The farmhouse is a square block, ashlar-faced building of dressed stone and is dated 1832.

Photographed by kind permission of His Grace The Duke of Northumberland.

The most impressive of the farm buildings (designed by John Green) is the west facing 'block' with the great pedimented gateway and beautifully symmetrical buildings either side.

Photographed by kind permission of His Grace The Duke of Northumberland.

Like the one at Warkworth, Belford Station was built 'on the grand scale'. Designed by Benjamin Green, c.1847, for the Newcastle and Berwick Railway Company, it, too, follows his usual Tudor style of architecture.

A bridge is known to have crossed the river, near the location of the present structure, as far back as the 12th century but, when this was destroyed, there was, subsequently, no bridge over the Tyne, north of Chollerford, for several centuries. The building of the present bridge, by John Green (1834-5), finally put an end to the dangerous practice of 'fording' the river.

It is interesting to note that the four, fifty-feet arches represented "a bridge of considerable magnitude" to the newspaper of the time.

The Charltons (- the foundation stone was laid on the 22nd August, 1834, by J W Charlton of nearby Hesleyside) were so pleased with the result that they recorded the designer, John Green, in an iron plate inserted in the battlement, at its opening on the 29th August, 1835.

Described as "an elegant road bridge, in honey-coloured sandstone".

It consists of three elliptical arches ('with pentagonal voussoirs and cornes de vache'), the centre one being 78 feet across and the two side arches each having a span of 63 feet.

Designed by John and Benjamin Green 1832.

An early 12th/13th century chapel that stood in Cambo was demolished in 1795. Eight stone, medieval grave covers, removed from the ancient site are now preserved inside the church. They were recovered by the Trevelyan family from their undignified situation as part of the fabric of a local farmer's barn.

Holy Trinity was designed by John and Benjamin Green, in 1842, for Sir John Trevelyan, at a cost of £987. The church is aisle-less with a four-bay nave. Green's original church had an entrance porch and a small bellcote, at the west end. The present tower and vestry were added by Sir Charles Trevelyan in 1884.

"Benjamin Green's stations, on the Newcastle to Berwick line", it has been written, "were generally much grander than those of the Newcastle and Carlisle Railway Company and are mainly neo-Tudor."

Chathill Station is dated 1847.

St Alban's Church stands on the site of a former medieval chapel: indeed, a village has been here since the Middle Ages.

Before 1250 the church was in the care of the monks of Tynemouth Priory who, in their turn, came under the ecclesiastic jurisdiction of the great Benedictine Monastery at St Albans. A very plausible theory suggests this may explain why Earsdon's Church is dedicated to Britain's first Christian martyr.

The church is Early English in style and measures seventy-nine feet long and thirty feet wide. It was built from the plans of John and Benjamin Green and was consecrated by the Bishop of Durham, on October 12th, 1837.

In the churchyard of St Alban's is an inscribed, granite obelisk, erected by public subscription and dedicated to the memory of the victims of the January 12th, 1862 Hartley Pit disaster, when no fewer than 204 men and boys – some only ten and eleven years old – lost their lives.

BLESSED ARE THE DEAD WHICH DIE IN THE LORD.
"IN THE MIDST OF LIFE WE ARE IN DEATH."
W. ALLAN. ACED 36
A. ATKINSON. ACED 20
W. ALDERTON. ACED 31
J. AINSLEY. ACED 19
J. ARMSTRONG. ACED 36
E. ARMSTRONG. ACED 12
J. ARMSTRONG. ACED 10
W. ANDERSON. ACED 17
J. BROADFOOT. ACED 19
C. BROWN. ACED 31
W. BROWN. ACED 25
S. BIRTLEY. ACED 24
S. BLACKBURN. ACED 26
H. CLOUGH. ACED 47
J. COUSINS. ACED 18
P. COUSINS. ACED 12
W. DIXON. ACED 27
R. DIXON. ACED 12
J. DOUGLAS. ACED 25
E. ELLIOTT. ACED 19
J. FOSTER. ACED 18
J. FOSTER. ACED 15
W. FAIRBAIRN. ACED 70
C. FAIRBAIRN. ACED 33
J. CALLACHER. ACED 32
D. CALLACHER. ACED 28

The Church of St Peter (Falstone, near Bellingham, Northumberland)

Falstone only became a parish in 1811, hitherto it was part of the very large parish of Simonburn.

In 1813, the discovery of a runic stone seems to indicate that the Angles arrived in the area sometime in the 7th or early 8th century and that Christianity had, indeed, taken root and perhaps even flourished in the Falstone area more than a thousand years ago.

There was a chapel in Falstone prior to 1541, though it appears to have fallen into disrepair.

In 1650, Parliamentary Commissioners recommended that "the Chappell at Falleston be rebuilded and made the Parish Church thereof": the recommendation was never implemented.

From 1709, rebuilding was undertaken and the Chapel was used, not by members of the Anglican community but by the Presbyterians.

A new church was built before 1725, within the graveyard of the present church, probably (it is avowed), just south of the present building; and it lasted, approximately, a century.

In 1824-5, "on the advice of a Greenwich Hospital agent", an entirely new church was built, following a public subscription and 'almost entirely modelled on H H Seward's churches at Greystead, Humshaugh, Thorneyburn and Wark'. St Peter's cost £1,040 and "the handsome rectory" a further £1,000. Seward, incidentally, was the 'house architect' to Greenwich Hospital (which had owned Simonburn since the execution of the Earl of Derwentwater for his part in the Jacobite Rebellion, of 1715. It is said that the churches were built largely to provide work for redundant chaplains after the end of the Napoleonic Wars).

They are described in "The Buildings of England: Northumberland" (1992 edition), as 'plain, lancet-style preaching boxes, typical of their period but well proportioned and provided with parsonages which form, with the churches, curious islands of urbanity in their wild, moorland setting'.

In 1879 the church was reseated and some restoration work was carried out but on the night of Sunday, November the 26th, 1882, the church caught fire (due, apparently, to the overheating of a flue), though because of the prompt action of the villagers, the resulting damage was not as serious as it might otherwise have been.

Eight years later, in December 1890, a second fire destroyed almost the entire church… "only the walls of the tower and the height of three or four feet from the main walls, escaping destruction".

The interior, the porch and the window tracery – all had to be restored: the remainder of the building is "original Green".

Notwithstanding this second, greater calamity the regular contributions from the parishioners of Falstone, together with subsequent generous gifts from various donors, meant that the 'new' Church of St Peter was rebuilt and reopened in May, 1892.

The interior, the porch and the window tracery were still restored after the fire of 1891: the remainder of the church is the work of John and Benjamin Green (1824-25).

A lovely, two-light, stained-glass, memorial window situated in the north wall of the nave.

Lord Redesdale commissioned the building of this picturesque little church, standing on a hill, overlooking the Rede Valley, about a mile south of Rochester. The church was built in 1844 (a date-stone set in the arch of the south porch entrance bears witness to this fact), by John and Benjamin Green: Lord Redesdale also endowed the living.

The Church is neo-Norman in style with a low apse.

The attractive west tower has a pyramidal roof.

Ingram Farm (Ingram, near Alnwick, Northumberland)

Described dismissively by Pevsner as 'by John Green' "but nothing special": probably of 1826'.

There is, in fact, a date stone set in the upper reaches of one of the farm buildings inscribed 'W.S.R. MDCCCXXVI'.

'W.S.R.' are the initials of William Spencer Roddam (though, strictly speaking, he was not a Roddam but a relation of the celebrated Collingwood family – he changed his name to Roddam by deed poll in order to inherit the estate). Born William Stanton Stanhope, he was the great grandson of Edward Collingwood (d.1783), the uncle of Admiral Lord Cuthbert Collingwood, of Trafalgar Fame. In 1821 the Ingram estate was sold to Trustees, under the terms of Admiral Roddam's will. The estate finally left the possession of the Roddam family in June of 1920.

The farm was submitted to auction in 1919 when, it is said, it received an offer of £26,000. However, the estate was withdrawn (- presumably the 'reserved price' had not been reached) though it was eventually sold the following year, by Lieutenant-Colonel Roddam John Roddam, of Glanton, to one Basil George Bryant. Robert Donkin (the father of eleven children) had moved to Ingram in 1806 and was given a tenancy of 65 years – he died, incidentally, on the 3rd of April, 1871, in his 96th year!

The date stone on the farm building confirms John Green's work in Ingram in 1826 but every indication suggests that the farmhouse (now Ingram House and owned by Lord and Lady Hill) is much older.

In his book "Reminiscences of Samuel Donkin" (one of Robert's sons), we read 'The windows of the farmhouse were lit up…' and the date referred to was 'Drifty Friday' (November the 18th, 1808).

The farmhouse was sold at the end of 1997. The house was advertised in the Newcastle Journal on November the 29th of that year together with the following extract from the agent's accompanying description:

"The original part of the house is believed to have been built *in the early 18th century* with further developments added later".

Assuming, as we must, that the description is accurate and that the writer obtained his information from an impeccably reliable source it seems safe to conclude that there was definitely a farmhouse on the site of the present building at least at the beginning of the 19th century and quite possibly a century before John Green was credited with adding the nearby sheds, barns, byres and stables; hemmels, granaries and storehouses.

Opposite Ingram House stands the more recently built Ingram Farm, to whom all the outbuildings on the other side of the road belong.

Its occupants are John and Sarah Wilson – to whom I am greatly indebted for much of this information.

The Wilson's are tenants of Lord James Percy, to whom the land belongs.

Nineteenth century farm buildings.

The date stone inscribed with the initials of William Spencer Roddam and the year John Green designed various farm buildings: MDCCCXXVI (1826).

Photographed by kind permission of John and Sarah Wilson.

The hemmels.

Photographed by kind permission of John and Sarah Wilson.

Ponthaugh Bridge (Lintsford, County Durham)

The bridge no longer carries main-road traffic having been bypassed by the A694.

Designed by John and Benjamin Green (1834-5) the bridge, with its two segmental arches and coped stone pillars to the approaches, crosses the river Derwent.

Situated at the top of Grey Street stands the imposing monument to one of Northumberland's greatest sons and built to commemorate the important contribution made by Charles, Earl Grey, KG, of Howick, to the eventual passing of the 1832, Great Reform Bill.

The 135 feet column was designed by Benjamin Green (perhaps from his brother, John Junior's earlier design) and was completed in August, 1838, at which time the thirteen feet high statue, sculpted by Edward Hodges Baily, was brought to the town from London aboard the Newcastle trading ship, Halcyon, and winched into position.

The Theatre Royal (Grey Street, Newcastle upon Tyne)

The present building, said to be "distinctly more Victorian than Georgian in the way it dominates the street and pavement", is Newcastle's second Theatre Royal.

The first was a Georgian, brick building situated mid-way along Mosley Street. This theatre was built by David Stephenson and opened on January 21st, 1788. It had a relatively short life and was demolished less than half a century after it was built to make way, in 1836, for Richard Grainger's Grey Street. The present theatre, by John and Benjamin Green, was started in July, 1836 and opened on February 20th, 1837: remarkably it was completed in less than eight months, though the portico was not finished until December of that year. Its first production was Shakespeare's "The Merchant of Venice".

Its magnificent portico has six, great, Corinthian columns, the two outer pairs rising from huge, moulded plinths. The columns support a triangular pediment containing the Royal Arms: carved by C J Tate of Newcastle, he was paid, we are told, eighty-five pounds for his craftsmanship and another five pounds for the stone he had used.

Corinthian pilasters frame the outer bays of the theatre's frontage, which project, rather like pavilions surmounted by balustrades.

The whole front is beautifully symmetrical in appearance.

The theatre's design is described as being "at one with the rest of the architecture in Grey Street". John and Benjamin Green, together with Grainger's own architects, are believed to be responsible for the more elaborate designs, both at the top of the street and on the west side of Grey Street: the simpler, 'less fussy' designs, on the east side, are said, usually, to be the work of John Dobson.

On November 24th, 1899, tragedy struck the theatre when the wonderful, period interior was destroyed by fire which gutted the whole theatre. Restored in 1901, the interior was again remodelled, at a cost of £6,333,000, in 1987.

Once more the theatre staged a 'grand reopening', on January 11th, 1988, with a wonderful performance of "A Man for All Seasons".

The Theatre Royal (Grey Street, Newcastle upon Tyne)

“This theatre is onc of thc largest and most beautiful out of London; as the portico projects completely over the foot pavement and is formed wholly of highly enriched stonework, it constitutes one of the greatest ornaments of Grey Street.”

(The Northumberland Directory: 1854)

The magnificent portico with its six, great Corinthian columns, the two outer pairs rising from huge, moulded plinths.

- the north side of the Greens' theatre block:

"The late Messrs. John and Benjamin Green designed the Theatre and the surrounding block." ('Veritas'; Newcastle Daily Chronicles: March 21st, 1868)

The decorative treatment of the main Grey Street frontage continues around the corner, on the wing, into Market Street. Then a plain section with two almost central Tuscan pilasters; a grand pavilion with five square columns followed by another plain section then, finally, a wing with Tuscan pilasters and first floor decorated windows to match the frontage on Pilgrim Street.

34-44 Pilgrim Street (Newcastle upon Tyne)

This is the rear end of the Theatre block and on grounds of both date and style it seems not unreasonable to suppose that it also was the work of John and Benjamin Green.

It has projecting wings, each with four, giant pilasters but no central pavilion.

Large decorative, pedimented windows are set in the first floor faces of the wings with the right wing having a tripartite window on the second floor. All three windows of the central bay are 'blind'.

- north side, facing south:

Originally both sides of the street contained houses above shops but after the disastrous theatre fire of 1899 the houses and shops along most of the north side were incorporated into the refurbished theatre, by Frank Matcham, the leading theatre architect of the period – c.1901.

Originally an office for the Newcastle Joint Stock Bank, on the east side of St Nicholas' Square, it was designed by Benjamin Green, c.1845.

Described by David Lovey as "an early Italian Palazzo-style finance house that set the style for the rest of Mosley Street".

The ground floor and first floor are rusticated. The first floor, with its five arched windows is surmounted by a rather grand balcony.

Ionic columns rise from the balcony, two storeys, to a heavily decorated, eaves cornice. All five windows on the second floor are pedimented.

The Literary and Philosophical Society (Westgate Road, Newcastle upon Tyne)

In 1775 the Philosophical Society was formed in Newcastle, followed, in 1813, by the Society of Antiquaries.

The Literary and Philosophical Society was founded in 1793 and was first based in the houseroom of the Dispensary, on Low Friar Street.

Around the year 1820, John Green ('the Nafferton carpenter') had abandoned his premises in Corbridge to establish himself, independently, as an architect in Newcastle.

In 1822, he received his first 'prestigious commission' when, in the face of strong competition, he was chosen to design the new premises for the Newcastle Literary and Philosophical Society, on Westgate Road: the Duke of Sussex laid the foundation stone and John Green was presented (by the Duke) with an inscribed silver trowel as a memento of the occasion. The building, a three-bay, two-and-a-half storey edifice has a north façade that has been described as "a fine piece of urban Greek Revival".

The entrance is set between two fluted, Doric columns 'in antis'.

The entire ground floor is rusticated. Above it, four giant, Doric pilasters support a Doric frieze and pediment.

Described by W W Tomlinson, in his "Comprehensive Guide to Northumberland", as "a large, sombre and impressive building", built (from 1822-5) at a cost of £16,000, on the site of the former town house of the Earls of Westmorland".

"As a specimen of architecture", adds Tomlinson, "the building will not rank so high as some large and ornate structures of more recent date… the façade is heavy and unornamented and draped in the 'sable stole' of accumulated coal dust (- Tomlinson was writing at the end of the 19th century). Several alterations and additions have, within recent years, been made to the building of this valuable institution, which has far outgrown the expectations of its original promoters."

The Literary and Philosophical Society (Westgate Road, Newcastle upon Tyne)

Photographed by kind permission of the Members of the Committee.

The Old Station (Norham, Northumberland)

Described in 'The Buildings of England: Northumberland' (1992 edition) as "the best surviving station on the Berwick and Kelso branch of the York, Newcastle and Berwick Railway company": *1851 by Benjamin Green.

The station house and offices are of only one storey on the platform side but (sometimes rather confusingly) two storeys to the rear, south side.

'The design,' adds Pevsner, 'is squared masonry with timber in-fill buildings along the length of the platform.'

The present owner, Mr Peter Short, is adamant that the station was built between 1847-49 and not, as Pevsner suggest, in 1851.

Peter began his career as a signalman but when the station finally closed on the 19th of March, 1965 he had the distinction of being Norham's very last Stationmaster – so perhaps his opinion on the date of its construction is worthy of consideration.

At the time of its closure the railway company employed two clerks, two porter-signalmen and five platelayers – as well, of course, as a Stationmaster. Shortly after its closure the 'scrap-metal vultures' descended on the station buildings, quite legitimately, to remove anything and everything of value. The actual rail tracks were fortunately spared the indignity and the lines were later sold to Belgian Railways.

The remaining, 1849, station buildings are those that are stone built: the others are correctly described by Pevsner as "timber in-fill buildings" the originals are the Stationmaster's house, the Porters' building and the Engine Shed. The latter was so called while the station was the property of the York, Newcastle and Berwick Railway Company but when ownership transferred to the North Eastern Railway Company it became a Goods Warehouse.

The building to the west of the Stationmaster's house consists of the Stable-block (right) and the Weigh-house: the stable had three stalls; two for Clydesdale horses (the property of the railway company) and one stall for the Stationmaster's pony.

Standing at the top of this building (as old photographs show) was the original signal cabin – the Porter's building

The present signal-box, built in 1900, stands on a brick tower with stone dressings

Despite the 'legal vandalism' that occurred in 1965 when authorised dealers stripped the station buildings of all their valuable metal fittings (fireplaces, etc) the 1900 signal cabin has been carefully and lovingly restored by Peter Short – as have several other buildings – and it is now a small museum containing, among a veritable cornucopia of other fascinating artefacts, the switches from the small station at Fallodon. Long since closed Fallodon was once the private station of Sir Edward Grey (created Viscount Grey in 1916), British Foreign Secretary from 1905-16.

The Passenger Warehouse was also built in 1900.

Other site buildings include a coal dept and a lime depot, or 'cells' later roof-covered so as to prevent falling rain damaging the lime.

Next to the stable-block, on its immediate right, there is a flight of stone steps leading up to the platform. Adjacent and parallel to the steps and at an angle of almost forty-five degrees there is now a four feet wide concrete incline. Instead of the concrete that is there today the 'incline' once consisted of a series of rollers lying on wooden sleepers. Boxes of rabbits, salmon, etc, were loaded onto the rollers where they were quickly and easily despatched from the platform to be collected by wagons waiting in the yard below.

The 1900 Signal Cabin.

Some of the buildings on the 'track side' of the station…

(far left, with the television aerial): The Station Master's House; then The General Room and Booking (Ticket) Office: the other half of this wooden structure (with the Telegraph sign) was the Station Master's Office:

The building on the right (with the 'Norham' station name-plate on the wall) was the Porters' Building: this replaced the 'rest room' to be seen just inside the entrance to the station yard.

Photographed by kind permission of Mr Peter Short.

The General Room & Booking (Ticket) Office, on the left; and the Station Master's Office (marked 'Telegraph').

Photographed by kind permission of Mr Peter Short.

Next to the Stable, on its immediate right, a flight of stone steps leads up to the platform. Adjacent and parallel to the steps, and at an angle of some forty-five degrees, there is a four feet wide concrete 'incline'.

When Norham was a working station and before the substitution of the concrete a simple roller contraption, on wooden sleepers, was used to transport goods (boxes of salmon, rabbits, etc) quickly and conveniently from the platform to be collected by wagons waiting in the yard below.

Photographed by kind permission of Mr Peter Short.

This part of the station consists of the Stable and the Weigh House.

The original Signal Box (or Cabin), of which there is now no trace, stood on the top of the Stable. It was very small and was no higher than the present chimney. It extended west only as far as the perpendicular (pink) pipe to the left of the first-floor window.

Photographed by kind permission of Mr Peter Short.

Outside the Weigh House (left) was the Weigh Bridge and while it is some time since this was removed traces of where it once stood are still faintly outlined in the ground in front of the ground-floor window.

Photographed by kind permission of Mr Peter Short.

The Lime Cells, or depot; roofed over at a later date to keep the lime dry.

The white building, on the left (at the far end of the railings) is the Passenger Warehouse.

The Engine-shed (from the station platform).

This was its original function and it remained so while the station was the property of the York Newcastle & Berwick Railway but when ownership transferred to the North Eastern Railway Company the engine-shed became a Goods Warehouse.

Photographed by kind permission of Mr Peter Short.

The Old Wesleyan Methodist Church, built in 1856-7, was designed by Benjamin Green and is now the offices of the Borough Treasurer. Situated on Howard Street it has a big front gable over three full-height arched panels. The doors on the ground floor are arched: the windows on the first floor are also arched but there is a nice tripartite window in the centre of the ground floor, between the two doors.

In the early days of the 19th century more than a thousand small sailing ships then belonged to the Tyne, with Master Mariners in command, not generally well provided for in their old age. In 1829 some of them banded together and set up a Friendly Society to provide pensions when they reached the age of sixty, or were incapacitated. It was decided to build a home at North Shields for elderly master mariners and their wives.

Built as Almshouses by John and Benjamin Green, between 1837-40, on land provided by the Third Duke of Northumberland (whose statue can be seen in front of the clock-tower) – for the Tyne Mariners Benevolent Institution.

Photographed by kind permission of the Tyne Mariners' Benevolent Institution: Hadaway & Hadaway, Solicitors (Reverend Timothy Duff); Secretaries to the Trustees.

The Sailors' Home, Borough Road,/New Quay (North Shields)

At the west end of Clive Street is the early 19th Century Market place or New Quay.

The former Northumberland Arms (now Collingwood mansions) was part of a scheme designed by the architect David Stephenson for the second Duke of Northumberland: the hotel was the five-bay centre block of a monumental twenty-one bay terrace.

To the right of the 'hotel' and around the corner into Borough Road is the Sailors' Home; added, in 1854-6, by Benjamin Green for the fourth Duke.

The east front, on Borough Road, is nine bays wide and four storeys high. The façade is clearly divided into three distinct sections each of the three bays. There are Ionic pilasters at either end of the building and the centre three bays are flanked by another Ionic Pilaster on either side. On the ground floor of the central section there is a central arched gateway with half-sized arched windows on either side. There are three full-size, twelve-pane, sash windows on the first floor the central one of which is pedimented.

The left and right 'wings' of the east front are identical.

Each, on the ground floor, has a central, half-size, arched window with full-size, twelve pane, sash windows either side.

The first floor windows are all full-size, twelve-pane, sash windows though the one in the centre has, what might loosely be described as an 'open segmental pediment'.

All nine windows on the third storey, across the entire width of the building are uniformly, twelve-pane, three-quarter size sash windows. All nine windows on the top storey, separated from those below by a cornice running the width of the elevation, are plain, recessed, half-size, twelve-pane, sash windows.

There is some rustication on the ground floor.

The south front of the Home, on New Quay, and overlooking the river, is very impressive.

Twenty-one bays from end to end, the 'left wing' is a replica of its right wing counterpart (the Sailors' Home) and has been carefully and exactly restored from what had become a derelict ruin.

The 'wings' are each eight bays wide: the 'hotel' centre section has five. The entire terrace is ashlar-faced and it has a rusticated ground floor. The three bays on the extreme right of the Home section are flanked by Ionic pilasters at either side. It is four storeys high though it looks as though, at some time, it may well have had a basement.

The windows on the top two storeys follow, exactly, the pattern on the east front. The five windows on the first floor, left of the three-bay section, are all full-size, twelve-bay, sash windows. Two of the three first floor windows between the pilasters are identical to those on the left; the centre window is a twelve-pane sash but, like the two around the corner, it too is capped by an 'open segmental pediment'.

There are five, half-size, arched windows on the ground floor between the pilaster on the left and arched gateway on the extreme left.

No longer a Sailors' Home the old building has been converted into luxury apartments.

The Sailors' Home (North Shields)

The façade on Borough Road is three-and-a-half storeys and nine bays wide, clearly divided into three sections by tall, Ionic pilasters.

The New Quay façade, facing the river and adjoining the old Northumberland Arms, is only eight bays wide.

No longer a Sailors Home the building has been converted into luxury apartments.

The former 'Northumberland Arms': now Collingwood Mansions.

Penshaw Monument (Penshaw, County Durham)

Erected in memory of John George Lambton, first Earl of Durham – so much a progressive in his day (he died July 24th, 1840) that the local miners christened him “Radical Jack”.

He owned the immense Lambton estates, had an income of some £80,000 a year, was a revolutionary Governor-General of Canada and an enlightened landlord ‘of the wide acres of which his monument is a fitting centrepiece’.

Local mythology suggests that the monument was erected by grateful tenants when ‘Radical Jack’ reduced their rents. Harry Thompson, in his book “Durham Villages” (Robert Hale, 1976) elaborates the myth, however, for when ‘Jack’ returned from “foreign wars” he declared that if they had enough money to spare that they could afford to waste it on such a useless object they could quite easily pay their rents and so promptly increased them to their former figure. Sorely aggrieved at this unexpected, not to say ungrateful reaction to this manifestation of their gratitude it seems almost unnecessary to add that the monument was left unfinished – minus the statue of ‘Jack’ on its summit!

A rather more restrained account of how and why the monument came to be built is given by Iris Wedgwood in her book “Northumberland and Durham” (Faber & Faber; 1932), who says “the monument was erected by local farmers in honour of the Earl of Durham, whose distinguished work in Canada laid the foundation of our colonial empire”. Some may view this as a somewhat exaggerated claim; nevertheless, as G M Trevelyan writes in his book “British History in the 19th century and after: 1782-1919,” ‘… the principle of complete self-government for Canada *was specifically the work of Lord Durham* who also, alone of the British statesmen of his day, seriously studied colonial problems from an Imperial point of view…”

Wedgwood continues: “It (the Monument) has earned the name of ‘the Farmers’ Folly’. To honour the return of their Lord the column was erected and the story goes on that the following year the harvest failed. The farmers are said to have applied to the Earl for a reduction of rent but he made answer that if they could build a monument ‘they could surely pay their dues’.”

Both of these accounts, by Thompson and by Wedgwood, bear a striking resemblance to another 'myth' – associated with the Percy Tenantry Column in Alnwick, Northumberland. This, too, is known as the "Farmers' Folly" and was erected in 1816 by the tenants of Hugh, the second Duke of Northumberland, 'in grateful recognition of his liberality in remitting their rents during a period of agricultural depression (the noble Duke had granted a reduction of 25% in rent after the Napoleonic war).

Thompson claims the Penshaw Monument is twice the size of its Athenian counterpart: Pevsner & Williamson ("The Buildings of England: County Durham") suggests it is only half the size.

In the late 19th and early 20th centuries hundreds of people, we are told, customarily flocked to view the giant obelisk each weekend throughout the Spring and Summer. In those far less safety-conscious times it was possible to climb a stairway to the top of the monument in order to enjoy the marvellous panoramic view. Unfortunately and inevitably a child fell from the 'roof' with fatal consequences. Immediately the privilege was withdrawn and thereafter climbing to the top of the monument was forbidden. Moreover, fences were erected to prevent people continuing the habit.

Visitor numbers began to dwindle alarmingly until, eventually, as a spectacle the Penshaw Monument was virtually ignored.

In the 1970s its future was uncertain: demolition was a distinct possibility, yet, still (in the year 2005) it survives and is the property of the National Trust, who have been its custodian for many years.

"It is in such classical bad taste", concludes Thompson, "it deserved to be retained.

The monument, which can be seen for miles around, stands on the summit of Penshaw Hill.

Designed by John and Benjamin Green it was erected in 1844.

The Greens based their design on the Theseum, in Athens – one writer claims it is twice the size of the original; another argues it is only half the size. It is Greek Doric in style though the columns are unfluted. Seven by four columns (each thirty-five feet high) with entablatures and pediments but neither roof nor walls. Originally, however, a stairway led up to the roof.

Photographed by kind permission of the National Trust.

Basically the work of John and Benjamin Green (1842).

The building is of ashlar; two storeyed with a balustraded parapet.

The north front (featured) has six arched windows, with rusticated surrounds on the ground floor, three either side of the main, two-columned entrance.

Above the entrance is a pedimented tripartite window and there are three, recessed, twelve-pane, sashed windows either side of it.

All the windows on the first floor have alternating pediments.

Photographed by kind permission of Mr Michael Rowland (Manager).

The (Lloyds) Trustees Savings Bank (Barrington Street, North Shields)

The east front has a narrow, two-columned porch with a small, pedimented window above it, to the left. The four recessed, arched windows on the ground floor are, like those on the north side, rusticated.

The four sash-windows on the first floor have alternating pediments.

Photographed by kind permission of Mr Michael Rowland (Manager).

Built of good ashlar stone by John Green, in 1831-32; later additions were made by Newcastle architect John Dobson, in 1848-49.

The Presbytery.

Built using good ashlar stone, by John Green in 1831-32; gabled and with castellated angle turrets.

Described as 'a plain building, situated near the Tyne, and surrounded by extensive grounds on all sides except the south (featured) where a beautiful lawn extends to the river's bank'.

Believed to have been built for one Charles Bacon (c.1820), Colvin attributes the house to John Green. The interior and wings were altered c.1965. To the rear there is a pretty little stable-block with cupola-cum-clock tower.

Photographed by kind permission of Major R H Dickinson.

Holy Trinity was designed by John and Benjamin Green, 1834-38.

It had a four-bay nave and transepts: tall, two-light lancet windows with Geometrical tracery.

When this photograph was taken (March, 2001) the church was being demolished and only the shell of a once beautiful building remained.

The church was built as a chapel-at-ease for the Church of St Michael and All Angels, at nearby Newburn.

The east side.

The nearby Parish Hall (of 1838) is quite probably the work of Benjamin Green. It has stone-mullioned, three-light windows with floating cornices.

Italianate and with a slender tower it was built in 1854-5 for the Mayor, A J Moore, by Newcastle architects John and Benjamin Green.

Photographed by kind permission of the University of Sunderland: Professor Peter Sidler, Vice-Chancellor.

Built between 1839-41 to the designs of John and Benjamin Green for the Duke of Northumberland, the church was consecrated on the 11th of August 1841. It served, for some twenty years, as a chapel-of-ease to Christ Church, the Parish Church of Tynemouth, which, though situated in North Shields, had been built in 1668 to be the Parish Church of Tynemouth when the Priory could no longer fill this role.

Holy Saviour ceased to be a chapel-of ease in 1861 when it was granted full parochial status. The building was enlarged in 1884.

The embattled west tower has been truncated but it is still 'an attractive' sandstone church with Perpendicular tracery in lancet-shaped windows'. The church has no aisles but it does have a hammer-beam roof.

The Old Tynemouth Railway Station (Oxford Street, Tynemouth)

The station, Tudor style, with a hitherto open porch, was designed by John and Benjamin Green.

In 1882 it was superseded by the current railway station which, in turn, became a part of the Tyneside Metro System.

For many years this fine stone building was semi-derelict, only being used as offices for a coal depot. The station was restored in 1986-7, when the early hotel (c.1847) and refreshment rooms, beside the platform, were replaced by a luxury development of retirement homes.

On the right of the building can be seen the old Booking Hall and Waiting Room.

This was the first railway station in Tynemouth.

It was opened on March 29th, 1847, by the Newcastle & Berwick Railway Company, whose coats-of-arms can be seen above the three arched windows of the portico.

One of Benjamin Green's most impressive, Tudor-style, railway stations designed and built for the Newcastle and Berwick Railway Company.

The Church of the Holy Trinity (Washington Village, County Durham)

A few yards to the north of Washington Old Hall and surrounded by trees stands the Church of the Holy Trinity.

Rebuilt in 1833 by John and Benjamin Green, in their Early English style, with flat ceiling and gallery, Holy Trinity stands on the site of an early medieval church. The only surviving relics of the ancient church are the west door arch and a Norman font with a shallow round bowl.

Generations of the Washington family must have been baptised in the font and to commemorate this fact and its association with the first American President the 'Stars and Stripes' (the flag of the United States) hangs above it.

The Red Cottage (Church Lane, Whitburn, County Durham)

The Red Cottage, Whitburn, was designed by Benjamin Green and built by Thomas Barnes, in 1842-3.

There are three date stones engraved with both the year and Barnes' initials, 'T B', to be seen in the brickwork – two on the north face of the house and one in the south garden wall.

The house displays a number of unusual exterior features, two of the most remarkable of which are to be seen on the east side of the house.

The cottage's twin gables overlook Church Lane. Crowning each of the two crow-stepped gables is a small chimney and it is to these one must direct one's gaze to observe what must surely be two of the most idiosyncratic features to be found among so many.

Standing perpendicularly atop the southern chimney is what is more usually and understandably mistaken for a lightening conductor rod but what is, in actual fact, a cricket stump; while nestling snugly and rather less obviously on the cap of its northern 'twin' is a cricket ball!

Why, when and how these two sporting artefacts come to be here is something of a mystery. The present owner is at a loss to explain their presence and is unable to say whether they were placed here when the house was built or whether a subsequent owner, who may also have been an eccentric cricket buff, mounted them simply as no more than a light-hearted, even frivolous, practical joke. But why these two particular objects when so many could so easily have been chosen? There seems little doubt they are meant to convey some obtuse message, a message clearly connected to cricket, but it seems extremely unlikely that after all these years we shall ever be able to appreciate its hidden significance.

Thomas Barnes was a man of substance (he also built and owned the nearby five-bay, Georgian, Whitburn House) who owned a local brickworks and his workmen built the Red Cottage to Benjamin Green's specifications, for their employer.

It is a quite extraordinary construction, unlike any other I have come across throughout my travels in both County Durham and Northumberland.

Standing observing and admiring the east face of the house from a position in Church Lane I am reminded, for some peculiar reason, of the witch's cottage, built of gingerbread and barley sugar and all kinds of sweetmeats, in Grimm's fairy tale of 'Hansel and Gretel'.

Yet, really, it *is* only the east façade of the house which creates this fanciful impression; the other fronts are far more 'conventional'.

Pevsner & Williamson, 'The Buildings of England: County Durham', describe the house as "an extravagant villa, in which the art of highly ornamental brickwork was consciously revived".

Though there are many features to absorb the attention the chimneystacks are the immediate centre of attraction. Tudor-style, they can, without any exaggeration, be reasonably described as works of art.

The diapered south garden wall is another distinctive feature and, despite its proximity to the sea and the inevitable and corroding effect of the ever-present salt air, this too has been preserved in near immaculate condition.

The south front with its crow-stepped gable on the right and lovely ornate Tudor-style chimney stack in the centre of the roof.

Photographed by kind permission of Mr Christopher Storey.

Crowning the smaller chimneys on the summit of each of the crow-stepped gables (either side of the street lamp in Church Lane) can be seen the cricket stump (left) and the cricket ball (right).

Photographed by kind permission of Mr Christopher Storey.

One of the moulded Tudor chimney stacks illustrates the incredible ornamental brickwork.

Photographed by kind permission of Mr Christopher Storey.

The Church of St Bartholomew (Whittingham)

The church is believed to have been founded around the time (737 AD) when Ceowulf, King of Northumbria, gave up his throne and entered the monastery on Lindisfarne, to be a monk.

The early Saxon church would consist, simply, of a tower, an aisle-less nave and a chancel.

The church would be as wide as the distance between the present north and south arcades and its height is reckoned to have been slightly greater than the eighteen feet archway at the west end of the nave.

(Facing the tower from the west, three feet or so from the tower to both right and left there are clearly to be seen two vertical lines of stones following exactly the same pattern as the quoins on the lower half of the tower. These two vertical lines are believed to make the western corners of the old Saxon church.)

Before 1840 the tower, with the exception of its battlements, was almost intact and exhibited the typical characteristics of Saxon work in these quoins and the rubble walling. The quoins, or corner stones, formed from local sandstone and still remarkably well-preserved, are arranged in a particularly unusual manner – a long vertical block of stone alternating with a short horizontal one, much wider and acting as a “bond stone” to bind the rubble walling of the tower to keep it together.

The quoins, it has been said, ‘are the best in the county’ and, indeed are of a style not only rarely found in Northumberland but unusual anywhere in the north of England.

But, in 1839-40, it was decided to pull down this beautiful and rather unique edifice and rebuild it “bigger and better” in ‘Gothic’ – a commission entrusted to the Newcastle architect, John Green: a decision made, moreover, not by the worthy villagers of Whittingham but by their newly appointed vicar, the Reverend Goodenough.

W W Tomlinson (“Comprehensive Guide to Northumberland”) describes the ‘restoration’ as “disastrous”. Nikolaus Pevsner et al (“The Buildings of England: Northumberland”, 1992 edition) calls Green’s work “vandalism”. In any event the destruction of the Saxon tower was mercifully not completed (the vertical lines of quoins on the south-west corner mark the point where the ‘vandalism’ stopped) and, thankfully, the lower half of the tower still remains and is linked to the west wall of the Saxon nave.

Inside the church the arch entrance into the tower, at the west end of the nave, is Saxon – similar to that in St Andrew's Church, Corbridge, built by St Wilfred and consecrated in 676 AD.

Its semi-circular arch and squared, heavy sides suggest a date of c.900 AD the way the stones in the walls are laid alternately, upright and flat, corroborate this date.

The Saxon archway was, for many years, blocked up enabling the tower to provide a safe refuge during the many Border conflicts. A strong door from the nave gave access to the tower. The archway remained blocked until 1909. Adjoining the Saxon work on the south side of the church is some 13th century walling, the lower courses of the aisle walls are medieval.

Over the past thousand years or more there have been numerous alterations and additions to this once simple church, resulting in the variety of architectural styles we see today.

The interior of the church is wholly in the Early English style. The Normans added a north aisle and arcade but, for reasons known only to himself, these were ruthlessly removed during Green's "alterations" of 1839-40. He replaced these ancient pillars and arches substituting imitation arches (- a copy of the 13th century arcade with its octagonal shaped pillars) in their stead.

The three-bay, south arcade and transept are genuinely late 13th century.

The south transept was heightened in the 14th century and re-windowed in 1840.

The south transept was formerly a chapel (or chantry) dedicated to St Peter, but all that remains now, below a trefoil-headed arch, in the south wall, is the old "piscina" – a basin for washing communion or mass vessels; provided with a drain and set in or on the wall south of the altar.

In the 13th century the chancel was enlarged, thus extending the Norman structure. Around 1725 another replaced the longer, medieval chancel. The remaining rounded uprights either side of the chancel arch are 12th century but the actual arch, alas, has gone – a victim to the chancel's further extension and "Gothicising", by F R Wilson, in 1871.

The church was dramatically altered by John Green in 1839-40.

The windows in the (1840 addition of) Lady Chapel and the clerestory and above the aisle in the north transept, have metal traceries "of bewildering variety".

The 13th century south chancel was heightened in the 14th century and refenestrated during the period of Green's alterations (1839-40): the metal traceries in the main south transept window are every bit as interesting and varied as those featured in the Lady Chapel.

The semi-circular arch entrance into the west tower with its squared, heavy sides suggest a date of c.900 AD.

The archway remained blocked until 1909.

The pillars in Green's north arcade are more clearly and sharply defined than their original 13th century counterparts in the south arcade.

On June 9th, 1829, the foundation stone of an intended bridge, over the river Tees at Whorlton, was laid by Miss Headlam, daughter of the Archdeacon of Richmondshire, 'amidst great rejoicings'.

But during a flood which occurred throughout the night of October 13th, 1829, the structure, or, to be more exact, as much of it as was already completed, was entirely carried away – the contractors being ruined as a consequence. On August 19th, 1830, the foundation of the north pier of a chain bridge was laid here and on April 1st, the following year, the main chains were thrown over the piers and safely moored into the rock on either side.

On July 7th, this elegant structure, erected from the designs of John Green was opened for public use: a band headed the procession followed immediately by the architect and the committee of management (all on horseback); then a train of twenty-seven carriages. Bringing up the rear 'a very numerous assemblage of spectators on horseback and on foot'.

Whorlton Bridge is the earliest suspension bridge, in the entire country, whose deck is supported only by its original wrought iron chains and stone piers. It has a span of some 173 feet.

The pretty little toll-house at the north end of the bridge is also believed to be the work of John Green.

Bibliography

I feel it is unnecessary to list every book referred to for useful information, during my researches. The following are those most frequently consulted and I am deeply grateful to the authors and their publishers.

A Memoir of John Dobson (Lambert & Co Newcastle, 1885): M J Dobson; Newcastle Town (Walter Scott, 1885): R J Charlton;

History of Northumberland, volume ii (1825): E Mackenzie;

History of Newcastle and Gateshead, three volumes (1884-7): R Welford;

Men of Mark 'Twixt Tyne and Tweed, volumes 1-3 (1895): R Welford;

History, Directory and Gazetteer of the Counties of Durham and Northumberland, volumes 1 and 2 (Edward Baines and Son, Leeds, 1827 a& 1828): W Parson and W White;

John Dobson, Newcastle Architect 1787-1865 (Tyne Publishing/Tyne & Wear Museums Service, 1987 & 2001): Faulkner & Greg;

The Buildings of England: County Durham/Northumberland (Penguin, 1983 and 1992): N Pevsner et al;

The Buildings of Grainger Town… (North East environmental Education Forum, 1997): David Lovie;

The Tyneside Classical Tradition: Classical Architecture in the North East (c.1700-1850) (Tyne and Wear County Museums, 1980);

Comprehensive Guide to Northumberland (W H Robinson, Newcastle): William Weaver Tomlinson;

History of Northumberland, various volumes (1840): John Hodgson;

Historic Architecture of Northumberland (1969): Allsopp & Clark;

Tyneside Classical (J Murray, 1964): Lyall Wilkes & Gordon Dodds;

P Lowery's article "William Newton – an Eminent Architect", in Tom Faulkner's (edn) "Northumbrian Heritage": special edition of Northern Architect;

Stewart Bonney's article "A New Direction for Dissington Hall", in the Northumbrian (issue 53, December 1999/January 2000);

Grey of Fallodon (Longmans Green & Co 1937): G M Trevelyan;

North Shields & Tynemouth: A Pictorial History (Phillimore, 1988): Richard Simpson;

The County of Durham (A & C Black, 1924): G E Milton;

Portrait of County Durham (Robert Hale, 1967): Peter A White;

Lost Houses of Newcastle and Northumberland (J Raines, 1996): Faulkner & Lowery;

An Historical, Topographical and Descriptive View of the County Palatine of Durham, three volumes (1834): Mackenzie & Ross;

The Old Halls and Manor Houses of Durham (F Graham, 1975): N Whittaker.